Torah Alive!

An Early Childhood Torah Curriculum

Lorraine Posner Arcus

URJ Press

New York, New York

It is a tree of life for those who hold fast to it, and all its supporters are happy. Its ways are ways of pleasantness, and all its paths are peace.

Proverbs 3:18, 17

Design by Dahlia G. Schoenberg

This book is printed on acid-free paper.
Copyright © 2004 by URJ Press
Manufactured in the United States of America

10   9   8   7   6   5   4   3   2   1

CONTENTS

• • • • • • • • •   Contents

Acknowledgments

Through the efforts of Rabbi Jan Katzew, Director of the Department of Lifelong Jewish Learning of the Union for Reform Judaism, *Torah Alive!* has become a reality. His vision of Torah education for young children connected me with this project.

Nancy Bossov, Director of Early Childhood Education at the URJ, brought this project from its infancy to maturity. Her treasure trove of experiences with young children, her creativity, and her organizational skills were precious assets to this project.

I am truly blessed to have many talented colleagues who are also my dear friends. They have graciously given me creative ideas, critiques, information, and support. Debbie Ellenbogen, Julie Thaler, Malka Kieffer, Nancy Eson, Meris Ruzow, and Marilyn Cohen are brilliant teachers who continue to inspire my teaching of young children. They have been my encouragement and my guides in creative teaching techniques. They provided me with valuable materials and information that were integral to this curriculum and to my teaching at the Bet Shraga Hebrew Academy, in Albany, New York.

I'm indebted to Mimi Brodsky Chenfeld, who has graced me by being a role model in the field of education for the young child. As the initial editor of this book, she generously shared the literary skills she uses as a renowned and prize-winning author of books and creative curriculum for early childhood educators.

Publication of this book would not be possible without the efforts of the staff of the URJ Press, especially Rabbi Hara Person, Ken Gesser, Michael Goldberg, Joel Eglash, Liane Broido, and Debra Hirsch Corman.

My wonderful husband, Ian, has patiently spent vacations and long car rides listening to books on tape while I quietly crowded the car seat with books to be researched and a laptop plugged into the cigarette lighter. As I typed away, he was always willing to pause his story to listen to mine. Together, we studied and discussed the Torah text, wrestling over difficult passages and finding a way to make them accessible to the reader. After thirty years, if that's not love, what is?

Thank you to my children, Rachel, Shira, and Josh, who have shared my classroom and continue to share my values and goals through their aspirations.

Finally, my deepest gratitude goes to my greatest teachers: my young students. I am grateful for the scholarly wisdom you share with me through your amazing questions and brilliant insights.

Introduction

Sitting by a tent constructed from a tablecloth draped over an easel, Joshua and Rachel are dressed as Avraham and Sarah as we are learning Torah in my early childhood classroom. Outside, children from the first grade are peeking in my room as they walk down the hall. I hear Shira. "Hey, I remember when I was Sarah. Do you remember when I had a baby when I was, like, ninety years old? They're so lucky they get to do this!" The first grade teacher comes out of her room, reminding her students that they were only sent to their cubbies to get their snack. What's taking so long!

*   *   *

Teaching Torah to young children is both exhilarating and challenging. It's my favorite part of the school day! Having the opportunity to be the facilitator of what is possibly a child's first encounter with a lifetime of Torah study is an awesome experience for me: using contemporary early childhood techniques to present an ancient text that has been handed down through the generations, touching the lives of every Jew . . . WOW!

This task, however, is not as easy as it may seem. While we might think of the Torah as a text filled with "stories," these are not necessarily lessons that are easy to present at this young age, or at any age. Tradition teaches that every story, every word, and every letter are written in the Torah for a reason. I like to believe that the Torah purposely deals with very difficult, delicate, and controversial topics so that we may address these issues in the context of a learning environment, whether it be in school, in synagogue, or at home.

The lessons and activities described in *Torah Alive!* are ones that I use in my own teaching of four-, five-, and six-year-old children at the Bet Shraga Hebrew Academy, in Albany, New York. There is always a level of excitement in my classroom as I take out new costumes and props in preparation for the next installment of Torah learning. "Who are we learning about today?" is a common question. As the children dress in their biblical costumes and place themselves among the background, scenery, and props of the particular story, they step into the Torah text, and the Torah comes alive!

Torah Alive! provides the teacher, students, and parents the opportunity to study Torah in a style appropriate for young children by confronting issues that we face in our lives every day, in a playful and creative manner. Through involvement in carefully prepared hands-on experiences with the stories from the Torah, young children are able to learn, along with teachers, friends, and family, from the experiences and lives of their foremothers and forefathers. As they experience the Torah text, God's wonders and our ancient history are brought into their lives. Each year, as students hear, learn, and discuss the same stories, bringing a year's worth of new personal experiences to a different learning environment, the discussion and the insights take on new meaning.

Through the use of the *Parent Connection*, teachers, students, and parents become partners in this exciting learning process. The parents of your students will never have to ask their children, "What did you learn in school today?" Instead, they will be able to say, "I know what you learned from the Torah today! Let's do a project together!" Parents, along with your students, will be eager to share the satisfaction and joy of acquiring new knowledge and insights through the study of Torah.

* * *

It's a hot day at the end of June in Albany, New York. The beautifully illustrated "Wall Torah" has been taken down and placed on the floor. The children sit on the floor around their artistic interpretations of the stories they have learned from the Torah. Candy is strewn across the artwork, reminding each child of the sweetness of Torah study. Struggling to sit on the tiny chairs of our classroom, surrounding the children, are kvelling parents, bursting with pride as each child answers questions about the lessons we learned from the Torah. With every question I ask, hands fly in the air. The parents are amazed at the amount of Torah the children have internalized. Our review is finished, and we roll up our Torah. We form a circle, dancing and singing through our tears, as each parent passes the Torah to his or her own child. The Torah has made its way around the circle. It has been lovingly kissed and hugged as it passes through the tiny hands and the larger hands. We end our celebration, thanking God for being able to share this special event in our lives. This has truly been a *Shehecheyanu* moment.

Guide for the Teacher

As it is taught: The world is sustained solely through the breath of children when they are studying.

Babylonian Talmud, *Shabbat* 119b

GETTING STARTED

The Torah (תּוֹרָה) is God's great gift to the Jewish people. Through the study of Torah, the children learn a set of relevant values and are provided with the opportunity to discuss sensitive feelings and issues.

Torah study for the young child should be vibrant and exciting. The Torah is filled with wonderful lessons, fabulous personalities, and enthralling events. Young children love stories. This curriculum, based on developmentally appropriate experiences for young children and my personal experiences in the classroom, capitalizes on their love of lessons taught in "story" form.

Children learn by doing. By re-creating the lessons from the Torah through their own dramatization, young students make it their own. The children readily identify with the biblical figures, and the Torah comes alive as the children become active participants in the weekly Torah lessons. If we imbue in our children a love of Torah study and surround their classroom with pictorial and artistic representations of the Torah lesson, the children are likely to develop a sense of the Torah as an integral part of their everyday lives.

THE TORAH: SACRED WORDS

The Torah, the first five books of the Bible, is also called the Five Books of Moses. It is written in Hebrew, on a scroll of parchment. Each end of the Torah scroll is attached to a wooden roller, called *eitz chayim*

(עֵץ חַיִּים). The Torah scroll is kept in the *Aron Kodesh* (אֲרוֹן קֹדֶשׁ), the Holy Ark, within the synagogue or place of prayer. Each week, we read a new *parashah* (פָּרָשָׁה), portion of the Torah. We read the first chapter on Simchat Torah (שִׂמְחַת תּוֹרָה), right after we have read the last chapter, completing the yearly cycle. Every year, we start again from the beginning, learning something new each time we study a familiar lesson. The Torah is the basis of Judaism and is an important way to learn the ancient history of the Jews and the values through which we live our lives.

As preparation for embarking on Torah study, one may teach about the physical qualities of the Torah: the *eitz chayim*, the parchment, how a Torah is written, who writes a Torah, the *rimonim* (רִמוֹנִים), or Torah crowns, when the Torah is read, where the Torah is kept, the difference between a Sephardic Torah and an Ashkenazic Torah. It is very exciting for children to see a "real" *sefer Torah* (Torah scroll). It would be wonderful to have a small *sefer Torah* in your classroom. Otherwise, every synagogue has Torah scrolls in the *Aron Kodesh*. Many synagogues provide stuffed toy Torah scrolls so young children can participate in the Torah procession, *hakafah* (הַקָּפָה), around the synagogue.

SACRED SPACE

If possible, designate a space in your classroom to be used only for Torah study. Just as the Torah has its own special place in the *Aron Kodesh* within the synagogue, the study of Torah should have its own place within your room. This will help prevent the children from confusing the events of the Torah with events of other ancient holidays such as Chanukah and Purim, or more contemporary celebrations, such as Yom HaAtzma-ut, that are not rooted in the Torah. Try not to teach these other lessons in that same space. From a bedsheet, create a backdrop for your lessons. If space is limited, hang a clothesline in a section of the room. Attach the scenery to the clothesline when needed, or push it to one side to take up a minimal amount of space. As you unfold the scenery, the children will recognize that it is time for Torah study.

PRESENTING THE LESSON: SACRED TIME

In preparation for each lesson, the teacher should first review the written materials. Presentation of Torah lessons usually takes approximately ten to twenty minutes. The duration of related activities will vary with their complexity. It is helpful for the children to begin their Torah study by sitting facing the scenery or backdrop. Reciting the *b'rachah* (בְּרָכָה), blessing, for studying Torah provides a sacred sense of connectedness with our heritage:

בָּרוּךְ אַתָּה יי אֱלֹהֵינוּ מֶלֶךְ הָעוֹלָם אֲשֶׁר
קִדְּשָׁנוּ בְּמִצְוֹתָיו וְצִוָּנוּ לַעֲסוֹק בְּדִבְרֵי תוֹרָה.

*Baruch atah Adonai, Eloheinu Melech haolam, asher
kid'shanu b'mitzvotav v'tzivanu laasok b'divrei Torah.*

We praise You, *Adonai* our God, Sovereign of the universe,
who calls us to holiness through mitzvot, commanding us
to engage in the study of Torah.

Before dramatizing the lesson, the teacher may want to provide a brief introduction to the story so the children can create a scene using their own imagination. This may be done the day before dramatizing the story or directly preceding the dramatization. Storytelling is an ancient Jewish custom. Capitalize on its magic when relating the lessons of the Torah to your students.

Some lessons may invite all students to wear costumes. At other times, the students will take turns being part of the audience or dressing as a Torah personality, always being reassured that they will get a turn soon. Young children generally love to "dress up." Catch the excitement as they role-play as these ancient and interesting personalities.

For purposes of dramatizing the lesson, the teacher will be the narrator or facilitator of the story. This will ensure that the children are hearing the story as true to the text as possible. After reviewing the appropriate materials and gathering the necessary costumes, scenery, props, and so on, the teacher will help the children dress as specific personalities and bring the individuals into the scene as the story unfolds. As the story is told by the teacher, the children will follow the action in mime and movement. The teacher may elicit dialogue through prompting, questioning, and directing. Generally, however, the teacher will need to recite all speaking parts, touching or looking at the person who would be doing the speaking. When God speaks in the dramatizations, the teacher should say, "And God said . . . ," then read the line in the dialogue, rather than pointing to any person or object. You may use the suggested dialogue/narration or create your own, trying to remain true to the text.

We have no photographs from biblical times. Instead, we need to consider the historical context of the stories from the Torah, as well as use our imaginations, to create the backdrops and clothing used to dramatize the teaching of the lessons. By using your imagination and creativity, the possibilities for meaningful experiences are limitless!

This curriculum is divided into thirty lessons. Torah study during the school year might begin a couple of weeks before Simchat Torah so that the children will be familiar with the story of Creation, *B'reishit*, for the Torah reading on Simchat Torah. Each teacher is encouraged to use the school calendar to shape and mold the yearly plan by expanding, consolidating, or reorganizing the chapters according to the needs of the class and the dictates of the Jewish calendar and the school calendar. For instance, you may find that you will teach the lessons relating to Moses when preparing for Pesach, necessitating taking lessons out of the sequence of the Torah. You might explain to the children that the lessons in every Torah are in the same sequence. While you may be jumping ahead to study about Pesach, you will return to the proper sequence after the holiday concludes. Keeping track of the order of the lessons through the use of the Wall Torah will provide a constant visual reminder of this order.

At all times, the lessons must be developmentally appropriate. Keeping in mind the ages and developmental level of the children in your class, you may want to enhance, expand, or modify the suggested lessons and related activities.

HOW TO USE THIS BOOK

Most lessons include the following:

- **Title** of the lesson in English, Hebrew, and transliteration (Hebrew sounds using English letters).

- **Picture** of how the students' dramatization of the Torah story might look in a classroom.

- **Introduction:** Background information providing the context in which the story takes place.

- **Synopsis:** A brief summary of the Torah story upon which the narration is based.

- **Cast** of characters for assigning parts for the dramatization.

- **Scenery, Costumes, and Props:** Suggested items to be gathered in preparation for the lesson. They help create the scene and tell the story.

- **Suggested Scene and Narration:** The suggested "script" to be used for the dramatization. You may enhance or modify it, being careful to remain true to the Torah text.

- **Discussion Questions:** Some of these questions will require factual recall. However, most of the questions are open-ended to encourage thoughtful discussions and insights. As you become comfortable with the curriculum, you will generate your own questions. Write them down, and add them to your book.

- **Puppets:** Suggestions for additions to the puppet bag to enhance the retelling of the current lesson. See pages 15–17 for more on the use of puppets.

- **Related Activities:** Suggested craft activities or group projects to enhance the lesson.

- **Wall Torah:** Suggestions for ways to fashion the class Wall Torah. See pages 13–15 for a complete description of the Wall Torah.

The book also includes:

- **Appendixes** including instructions for a recipe and dances. There is also a list of useful Web sites for early childhood education and Torah study for young children and adults. The Web sites are particularly useful for teachers and parents who wish to gain greater insights into the Torah lessons.

- **Glossary of Hebrew Terms**, written in Hebrew characters, transliteration, and translation.

- **Bibliography and Resources** with suggested books to read and/or display when teaching about various Torah personalities.

Torah Alive! also includes two companion books and a CD. Music is an integral part of the curriculum, and *Music Connection* provides great songs for each lesson and helpful suggestions for how to use them in the classroom. The book includes a CD.

Parent Connection is a companion book for parents. The *Parent Connection* contains the same **Introduction** and **Synopsis** as the teacher's guide, so parents will have the same information as the teacher. The **Discussion Questions** and **Related Activities** are parallel but different from those used in the classroom. Many of the questions and activities relate to the child's family or environment. You may encourage children to share with the class the projects or discussions in which they engaged with their families. After each lesson is introduced and presented in class, the parents should be notified to begin their preparation, activities, and discussions at home. A sample letter to parents can be found in Appendix C on page 239.

In a typical classroom, a week's lesson begins on day one with the dramatization of the Torah story. Dress children in the necessary costumes and present the scripted or original narration. When finished, pose the discussion questions to the children and conduct a discussion. At the end of day one, send home a letter to parents to let them know a new lesson has been introduced.

On day two, review the previous day's learning and link it to one of the related activities.

For day three, gather and prepare materials for the Wall Torah. Review the Torah story, generate ideas from the children of how to depict it, and have the children create their contributions to the Wall Torah.

On day four, guide the children in fashioning clothing and props for use with the Torah puppets. Review the story with the children as each child uses his or her own puppets, or children form small groups with their classmates, to act out the story.

Finally, on day five, prepare an additional related activity to complete the lesson.

QUESTIONS: SACRED DISCUSSION

"The Torah has seventy faces," and we are invited to interpret it.

B'midbar Rabbah 13:15

After presenting the dramatization, invite the children to ask their own questions. Young children are regarded by theologians as being some of the best students of Torah. Invite them to offer their interpretations. The open-ended discussions conducted at this age will be an introduction to the way Torah study is conducted throughout one's life. Create an atmosphere in which Torah study is an exploration and discussion, not just storytelling. Encourage your students to question and ponder the lessons from the Torah. Keep a chart or book of great questions asked by the children. Invite a local rabbi or other resource person to visit and discuss these questions. Every year, the questions will change! The questions provided in this book, at the end of each lesson, are only a suggestion to be used as a springboard. When developing your own set of questions, be sure to include ones that are open-ended, sparking curiosity and critical thought, along with those questions that recall facts.

When asking factual questions, refer to the synopsis included in the chapter or the Torah text for correct answers. Questions suggested in this book that contain phrases such as "Why do you think . . . ?" or "What do you think . . . ?" may not necessarily have "correct" answers. Try to be accepting of all children's ideas. There are students and scholars who spend their lives discussing and answering some of these questions. If a student's response appears to be totally off base, you might answer,

"That's an interesting point. Does anyone have a different idea?" You may then proceed to have further discussion on an answer that appears to be more reasonable.

"DID THIS REALLY HAPPEN?"

Often, the children will ask, "Did this really happen?" A simple and accurate answer would be, "This is how it is written in the Torah." Every Torah is exactly the same. From this text, we learn lessons and values that guide our lives.

It is important to recognize that Jewish tradition doesn't portray any individual as being exclusively good. The personalities in the Bible were subject to human frailties, made mistakes, and may have used questionable judgment. We acknowledge their mistakes and learn from them. Additionally, the events in the lives of these leading biblical characters illustrate that despite mistakes, a person can still travel in the path of God.

PICTURES

Keep a camera handy. The children love seeing themselves in their biblical roles. It brings the lessons and the personalities to life! You can create books from the pictures by adding dictation or original writing from the children. If using a digital camera, you can send pictures of each lesson electronically to the parents or post them on a school Web site.

COSTUMES

The events in the Torah take place in a very warm part of the world, in the Middle East region. In ancient times, both men and women wore long robes and covered their heads for protection from the sun and perhaps for reasons of modesty. People of greater prosperity wore more ornate clothing. Fabrics were dyed with natural materials and may have been very bright and colorful.

Each time the children are dressed as the personalities from the Torah, they may wear long robes and a head covering. The Matriarchs and Patriarchs, our leaders, may have been dressed in more ornate clothing. Consider reversing gender roles for purposes of these lessons.

Early childhood teachers are accustomed to recycling old clothing and fabric and creating exciting and meaningful costumes. Someone's rags will become a cherished addition to your collection! This will create a wardrobe of costumes for years to come. Enjoy constantly enhancing and modifying your inventory.

Clothing

You may collect adult-sized new or used T-shirts, old nightgowns, and pajamas. They are perfect for the long robes worn by men and women of biblical times. Long robes and vests can be easily fashioned from large pieces of all different kinds of fabric or old pillowcases. You may also fashion a "no sew" pinny:

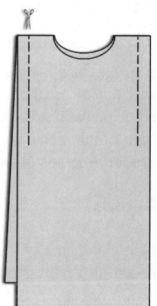

1. Cut a piece of fabric approximately 12 × 48 inches.

2. Bring short sides together, folding in half.

3. Cut small semicircle for head opening on folded edge.

4. Cut a slit on folded side, 1 inch from each edge.

5. Continue to cut or tear down fabric for approximately 10 inches. Cut the folded end of the strip of fabric open and tie the sides to form a robe.

For "furry" costumes, fleece, terry, velour fabrics, or the old fur lining to a coat work well. For animal costumes, fabric stores generally carry a selection of fabric designed to look like the skin of various animals.

Several stories include a camel. The head of a camel can be attached to a hat, or a camel head could be fashioned from a large paper bag. The child's body could be covered with brown fabric or a pinny.

Ask parents and caregivers to send in old bathrobes, tunics, choir robes, etc. These can all be cut to size for the children. Enlist the help of families to do small amounts of sewing. Embellish the robes with trim, sequins, or small pieces of fabric. Apply with craft glue or hot glue.

Head Coverings

Desert dwellers covered their heads to protect themselves against the hot sun. A rectangular piece of fabric, approximately 12 × 14 inches, will work well. A wide band of elastic or a strip of fabric tied in a knot will hold the fabric on the child's head. You may also attach the elastic, in a loop, to the front of the rectangle across the center 6 inches. For the girls, you may use large scraps of sheer fabric held on with a band of elastic sequins.

Beards

Men in the time of the Torah probably had beards. You can purchase a beard at a party store or fashion one from furry fabric. You'll want a brown or black beard for a young man and a gray or white beard as the personalities "age."

Cut a triangle from the fabric, and attach elastic to two corners. Put the beard under the child's chin and the elastic behind the ears and on top of the child's head.

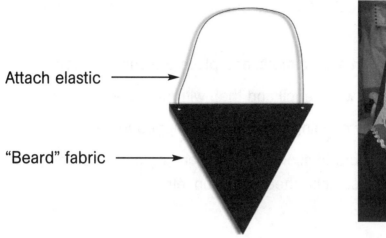

Attach elastic ———→

"Beard" fabric ———→

SCENERY

Backdrops

By having a backdrop that might resemble the scenery of the lessons from the Torah, the children are able to visualize the setting. Backdrops may be switched for each new setting. The children will enjoy making the scenery. Before fashioning each backdrop, discuss with the children what that scene might look like. For example, ask the children:

- What does a desert look like?

- What kind of trees would we find in the desert?

- Where do you find water in a desert?

To create a backdrop, collect a white or light blue flat bedsheet, tempera paints, and sponges:

1. Cover the floor with a drop cloth, and place the sheet on top.

2. Outline the design with pencil and then with permanent marker.

3. Paint the design by dabbing with sponges dipped in paint.

4. Attach strips of Velcro to allow for interchanging parts. You may want to add pictures of camels, sheep, the sun, etc.

Props

The people of the Torah lived in tents. An A-frame piece of climbing equipment can be a very versatile prop. Drape the A-frame with an old tablecloth or a large piece of fabric. A painting easel will work well too.

Many of the lessons involve the use of a tree. Trees can be created by using large tubes such as those from carpeting. Cut out large palm leaves from construction paper, and attach them to the inside of the tube on the top. An old coatrack with leaves attached will also work well.

Many lessons take place at the well, the center of social activity in ancient times. Measure a large piece of paper, plastic, or shower curtain to go around the outside of a large trash can. Draw rocks on the paper, or cut them out from gray paper and have the children color and affix them to the larger paper. When needed, wrap the large paper around the trash can and attach with tape. Fold and save the "well" paper for future use.

A fire may be made from an open box standing on its short side. Fill the box with yellow and orange tissue paper. Depending on your region and climate, logs and pieces of wood may be used to suggest a campfire.

STORAGE

A set of shelves, an old trunk, large suitcases, or a portable closet would make a great storage unit for the costumes. As your collection grows, you may want to separate the different types of costumes (e.g., robes,

head coverings, fur). The children will anxiously await each new lesson as you take out new combinations of costumes.

WALL TORAH

As each section of Torah study is completed, the children love to create a mural depicting the story. The murals are created in a collage style. Start the process by discussing with the class what needs to be included in the mural to best describe the story. Each child decides what to draw. Cut out the individual pictures, and affix them to the mural paper with glue. Use a variety of art media to enhance the murals. Use scraps of fabric or wallpaper for clothes and tents. Help the children to create a background for the scene. Add mountains, sand dunes, trees, animals, the sun, birds, and so on. Embellish and enhance murals with marker, crayon, paint, and glitter.

The suggested components for each Wall Torah segment described will help you the first time you undertake this project. These are only suggestions. It's exciting to develop your own style. Each year, the Wall Torah develops its own character as you find new and different techniques or art media.

Special Paintbrush

A wonderful, quick, and fun way to add grass, bushes, and trees to your murals is through the use of a special paintbrush you can create easily using recycled materials. You'll need:

- A cylindrical object such as an old capped marker

- Several rubber bands cut into 1-inch pieces

- A 4-inch strip of masking tape

Place the cut rubber bands evenly along the sticky side of the masking tape, extending over only one edge of the tape . Wrap the masking tape around the last inch of the marker. Trim the rubber bands, if desired. The painting implement will look like a tree. To use this paintbrush, put the desired colors of paint in a dish. Dab the brush in the paint(s), and then dab it on the paper in a quick motion, constantly changing position so you get the effect of leaves or grass. In an instant, you'll create the effect of foliage.

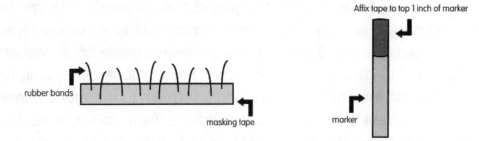

Displaying the Wall Torah

If desired, write a description at the bottom of each picture. The murals can be displayed on the wall and wrapped around the room, building as the year progresses. Try putting an *eitz chayim* on the wall at the point where you begin your Wall Torah, keeping in mind that the Torah is read

from right to left. The mural describing the lesson on *B'reishit* will be affixed to the left of the *eitz chayim*. Estimate how far around the room your Wall Torah will reach. Place the second *eitz chayim* at that point to give the children a sense of how much they will be learning from the Torah. The children will gain a sense of the order of the lessons, as well as a feeling of being enveloped by the beauty of the Torah. A roll of paper, 24 inches wide, works well. Cut each mural approximately 24 × 36 inches. Some lessons may only require half a page. The pictures included are only an example. Create your own style and technique!

TORAH PUPPETS

Another fun way to involve all children in role-playing as Torah personalities is for the students to design their own "Torah puppets" to be used throughout the year. As new personalities are presented, they add appropriate props and clothing to their puppet bags. Use of the puppets will provide an additional opportunity to review the Torah lessons. Puppets are ancient resources for learning as well as for enjoyment. Be sure to let the children have opportunities to use the puppets during a free-choice time. This is the time for children to create their own dialogue and narration. With encouragement from the teacher, you'll be surprised to hear how closely they imitate the original presentation of the lesson.

Each child makes a male and a female puppet. As they review the lessons, they will form small groups to have enough puppets to dramatize a particular lesson. The size of their groups varies according to the number of puppets needed to dramatize a particular story. In each chapter of this curriculum, there will be a list of items to add to each child's collection of props, stored in a puppet bag. This simple style of puppets allows the children to express their own imagination by having the freedom and ability to change the look of the puppets for each new lesson.

To make puppets, you'll need:

- Slats from old mini blinds, paint stirrers, or old rulers

- Felt of varying skin tones

- Wiggly eyes from a craft store

- Hair created from yarn, fibers from *etrog* box padding, or doll hair purchased at a craft store

- Tagboard (railroad board)

- Tacky glue or hot glue

- Markers

- Large paper clips or strips of Velcro

- Gallon-size resealable bags (bags with sliders are easier for the children to use)

1. Cut strips from mini blinds 10–12 inches long. (Save the strings that hold the blinds together. You will use them as "ladders" during the Yaakov lessons.)

2. Trace the end of a paper cup, about 2 inches in diameter, on the felt, and cut out to make faces.

3. Trace male and female bodies onto tagboard (see page 17). Cut them out.

4. Staple the heads and bodies to the mini blinds.

5. Affix wiggly eyes with tacky glue or hot glue. Staple or glue the hair.

6. Have the children draw facial features with markers.

7. Attach a large paper clip or strip of Velcro to each shoulder. The clothing will be slipped under the paper clips or attached with the Velcro.

8. Store puppets in resealable bags.

Costumes and props are listed in each lesson. Unless there is a specifc suggestion, clothing may be fashioned from such materials as construction paper, fabric, wallpaper, or wrapping paper.

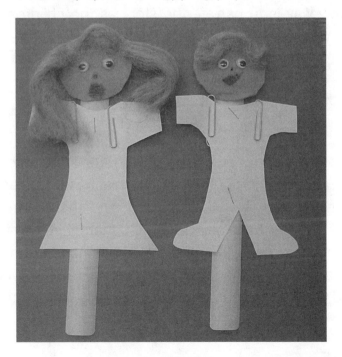

ORIGINAL BOOKS

Books created by the children are wonderful ways to reinforce and review the sequence of events in the Torah lessons. This is very easy to do if you have access to a binding machine. Otherwise, the books can be bound with various types of clips. Books may circulate among the families, each child borrowing the book for one night. Invite families to write comments to indicate they have read the book. It's a great way for the families to become involved in the Torah study.

One way to create the book is to review the sequence of events by having the children dictate the story, each child dictating one important concept and then illustrating his or her contribution. Another way to create the book is by taking photographs as you are presenting the lesson. Affix each picture to a separate page, and ask the children to provide the narration and dialogue for the pages of the book. Children may also write the narration using inventive spelling or by copying the words.

TORAH VIDEO

Children will enjoy creating a video of their lessons from the Torah. This may be done as a review at the end of the year or as each story is completed. An easy way is to narrate the story as the children pantomime. You may also want to rehearse some brief lines with them.

SIYUM

It's party time! A wonderful culminating event for the study of Torah is a *siyum* (סִיּוּם), a celebration of the learning that has occurred throughout the year. Take the Wall Torah down, and seat the children around it. Spread candies on the Wall Torah to remind them that the study of Torah is sweet. As the children answer simple questions about the Torah lessons, they take a candy. When they are finished, roll the Wall Torah and dance around with it to prepared music or singing. Inviting the parents to

participate in this event is a great opportunity to involve the parents in this exciting learning process.

APPROPRIATE LITERATURE

A bibliography has been provided that includes a list of suggested, developmentally appropriate books. This is certainly only a partial list of available age-appropriate literature. When selecting books that are not on the list, make sure they reflect a Jewish perspective on the Bible before sharing them with the children. For example, many children's books illustrate God as an old man. There are many ways to "see" and "feel" God. Through the beautiful creations in nature, Jews can see and feel God. A book ascribing a human form to God through illustrations would not be an appropriate choice and would limit the children's abilities to develop their own individual perspective. It is also important to make sure the books you choose remain true to the Torah text or the midrashic literature.

WHAT IS MIDRASH?

There are many events and stories in the Torah where we feel we may need to "fill in the gaps" or provide answers that are not directly addressed in the story. There is a wealth of stories, each called a midrash (מִדְרָשׁ), that were written over many years by the great Rabbis, scholars, or contemporary authors. These are stories that are not directly from the Torah but help to answer questions that may arise. They enhance the scenarios that seem to need more information. The story of Avraham and the idols is an example of midrash. The Torah does not tell us about Avraham as a child. This midrash was developed to help us understand Avraham more fully. Make sure when citing a midrash that the children are aware that the story is not contained in the Torah.

WHAT ABOUT THE WOMEN?

Children frequently ask, "Why aren't there any girls in this story?" or "Why does God talk to the men so much?" We can't change the contents of the stories from the Torah, but we can make sure to emphasize the critical role of the women. While we adults may have the desire to conjecture about the role of women who are not directly mentioned in the Torah lesson, we must be careful to remain true to the text and not to teach the children anything they will need to "unlearn" at another point in their education. You may tell the children that there were certainly many members of the community who were present, yet not directly mentioned in the Torah. You may also mention that the events of the Torah happened a long time ago and that men and women had different roles than they do today, when women and men have equally important roles and jobs.

SUGGESTIONS TO KEEP IN MIND BEFORE YOU START

- Take a deep breath! Teaching a new curriculum is a process.

- This curriculum is a "suggestion." Make it yours by adding your own touches and ideas. Balance this curriculum with your own skills and strengths and those of your students.

- Be flexible. The curriculum will change, evolve, and grow from year to year.

- You may not want to do every activity suggested in each of the lessons in one year. For young children, this is only the start of a lifetime of Torah study. You may be able to share and coordinate aspects of the curriculum with colleagues teaching another grade.

- Capitalize on your young students' love of stories, role-playing, questioning, giving opinions, and art projects.

- Take time to prepare thoroughly. Even though I may teach the same lessons year after year, I take the time before each lesson to make sure that I am familiar with the contents of the text and the lesson and the terminology that I will use. As I become more comfortable and more relaxed, I am able to be more animated and more enthusiastic.

- Sometimes our students are our greatest teachers. Be willing to learn along with your students. Young children have great ideas and a thirst for new materials and techniques.

THE TORAH AND OUR CONTEMPORARY LIVES

Learning Torah is an ongoing process. We study Torah throughout our lives. Each time we study a passage or story, even if we have studied it before, we learn new insights, generate new questions, and find new ways to relate those teachings to our everyday lives.

In the course of the academic year, there will be times in your classroom when either ordinary or extraordinary events will occur. Seize the opportunity to use teachings from the Torah to solve a problem or relate to something wonderful that has occurred. For example, a guest may come to visit your classroom. We learn from Avraham and Sarah how to treat our guests.

Teaching Torah to young children is an exhilarating experience. Enjoy the process and watch the Torah come alive!

LESSONS 1 AND 2

Creation
בְּרֵאשִׁית
B'reishit

Genesis 1:1–2:3

INTRODUCTION

The story of Creation, the first *parashah* in the Torah, is read on Simchat Torah and the following Shabbat. A suggestion would be to time this lesson to begin during Sukkot (סֻכּוֹת) so the children are familiar with the Creation story in time for Simchat Torah. Continue the lessons by finishing the related activities after Simchat Torah.

My favorite way to introduce the story of Creation is to gather a variety of books on the subject and see how different artists interpret the same text. Often the children ask, "How could this happen in a day?" "What about the dinosaurs?" A simple answer is, "There are many versions of the story of Creation. This is how the Torah teaches us about Creation."

B'reishit (בְּרֵאשִׁית) is the first word of the Torah, as well as the Hebrew title of Genesis, the first book in the Torah. The word *B'reishit* can be translated as "When [God] began [creating]. . . ." This *parashah* describes how, for the first time, God created all that there is in the world. We can see for ourselves, however, that God continues the miracles of "creating" all the time.

Using one of the many beautiful books suggested in the bibliography, the children learn that there was an order to Creation and that God was proud of all that was created. God even created a day for us to rest.

SYNOPSIS

When God began to create the heaven and the earth, there was chaos and darkness and only God's spirit moved throughout the emptiness.

God said, "Let there be light"; and there was light. God saw that the light was good and separated the light from the darkness. God called the light Day and the darkness Night. And there was evening and there was morning, a first day.

God said, "Let there be a separation of the waters, water below and heavens above." And it was so. God called the space between the waters Sky. And there was evening and there was morning, the second day.

God said, "Let the waters gather together so dry land may appear." And it was so. God called the dry land Earth and the waters Seas. And God saw that this was good. And God said, "Let the earth grow flowers, trees without fruit, trees with fruit, and all types of vegetation." And it was so. And God saw that this was good. And there was evening and there was morning, the third day.

God said, "Let there be great lights in the sky to separate day from night; they will set the times for days and years." And it was so. God made two great lights: the larger light, the sun, to shine in the day, and the smaller light, the moon and the stars, to shine at night. And God saw that this was good. And there was evening and there was morning, the fourth day.

God said, "Let there be fish in the water and the birds in the sky." And God saw that this was good. God blessed them, saying, "Be fertile and increase." And there was evening and there was morning, the fifth day.

God said, "Let there be every kind of animal on the earth." And it was so. And God saw that this was good. And God said, "Let us make man. They shall rule the fish, the birds, the cattle, the whole earth and all the animals." And God created man and woman in God's image. God blessed them and said, "Be fertile and increase. Fill the earth and rule all the animals." And it was so. And God saw all that had been created and found it very good. And there was evening and there was morning, the sixth day.

The heaven and earth were finished. God rested on the seventh day. God blessed the seventh day and declared it holy because God ceased from all the work of Creation.

SUGGESTED SCENE AND NARRATION

To introduce this lesson, choose two or three wonderful books about Creation from the bibliography. You may have the children hold them open and turn the pages as you describe each "day." As you read from the books, point out how different artists interpreted this story.

After discussing the order of the days of Creation, you may also review this story through creative movement. Choose a selection of music that provides you with the sensation of quiet and emptiness, leading to the excitement of Creation. The sound track from *Fantasia* is an example of a good source.

Before playing the music, cover the children, as they crouch very low, with a large bedsheet, cloth, or parachute. As the music increases in intensity, individual children may emerge from the covering and move, representing the light, dark, water, trees, flowers, sun, stars, birds, fish, animals, people, and so on. There are many variations in this activity. Children may choose their "day," they may be given props to move as a specific "day," or they may all move as each day and come back to the covering of the sheet as each day ends and get ready for the new day.

DISCUSSION QUESTIONS

• Why do you think Creation happened in this order?

• Why did God create humans after all the animals?

• Why did God create Shabbat last?

• What kinds of things do we see every day that are signs that God continues the process of Creation?

RELATED ACTIVITIES

Personal Torah for Simchat Torah

This project may require more than one day.

1. Start with a piece of copy paper 8½ × 14 inches. With a marker, draw a line through the center of the long side. Divide the long width into four equal segments. You now have two rows of four boxes.

2. On the top row, starting at the left corner, write "Day 1" through "Day 4." On the bottom row, starting from the left corner, write "Day 5," "Day 6," "Shabbat." Make one copy for each student.

3. Write each student's name in the bottom right box.

4. Use the other seven boxes to illustrate the story of Creation. First, you may show the children how other artists interpreted the scene. Then invite them to draw their own.

5. When students have finished the illustrations, cut the papers along the long line. With clear tape, join the two pieces to form one long 28 × 4–inch piece.

6. Attach each end of the paper to an old-fashioned clothespin, keeping the rounded side of the clothespin on top. The clothespins are the *eitzei chayim*.

7. Roll the scroll from both sides into the center. Hold together with a ribbon or rubber band.

8. Cut a rectangle from felt or fabric to use as a Torah cover. Make sure the rounded edges of the clothespin stick out. Decorate with glitter, sequins, or markers. Tie with a ribbon.

9. Dip the rounded edges of the clothespins in glue and then in silver glitter to look like the crowns (*rimonim*) on the Torah. Dry flat so the glitter doesn't drip off!

Class Book of Creation

Using the same suggestions for depicting each day as described in the Wall Torah section on pages 28–29, create a classroom book of Creation. You need approximately eight sheets of heavy white paper or tagboard. The page for each day is smaller than the next. (It is fashioned like *The Very Grouchy Ladybug*, by Eric Carle.) Cut the pages as follows:

- Shabbat: 9 × 12 inches (full page)

- Day 6: 8½ × 12 inches

- Day 5: 8 × 12 inches

- Day 4: 7½ × 12 inches

- Day 3: 7 × 12 inches

- Day 2: 6½ × 12 inches

- Day 1: 6 × 12 inches

- Cover: 5½ × 12 inches

Draw a thin black line ½ inch in on one of the 12-inch sides of each paper. Line the pages up and write the "Day" in the center of the ½-inch space that shows on each page. (If using a binding machine, punch the holes before the children add their artwork to the pages.) When fashioning the individual pages, the children should not go below the black line. The children may work together to create one page. The children will love reading the book in class, or it may circulate among the families.

WALL TORAH

Divide the 24 × 36–inch mural paper into seven sections. Invite the children to create part of each day of Creation. (These are only suggestions. Encourage the children to generate their own ideas.)

- **Day 1: Light and dark.** Give each child a piece of light paper and a piece of dark paper to tear in several pieces. Put glue on the mural paper, and let the children affix the torn paper.

- **Day 2: Separation of the waters.** Cut white, light blue, and dark blue tissue paper into small squares. Put glue on the top and on the bottom of the space for Day 2, leaving the "Separation" in the middle. Glue crumpled white and light blue paper on top. Glue crumpled light and dark blue paper on the bottom.

- **Day 3: Land, flowers, and trees.** Cut several different colors of tissue paper into small squares. Draw many vertical lines (stems) of differing heights in the Day 3 space. Put dots of glue on the top of each stem. The children glue one piece of tissue to form a flower. Glue a crumpled piece of a second color in the center of each flower. Glue crumpled brown and green tissue on the bottom for grass and land.

- **Day 4: Sun, moon, and stars.** Draw a circle (sun) with glue in one corner of the Day 4 space. Have the children sprinkle it with gold glitter. Repeat the process to make a moon using silver glitter. Give each child a strip of adhesive stars, and have them fill the rest of the space with stars or draw stars with markers or glitter.

- **Day 5: Birds and fish.** Cut a piece of dark blue tissue paper to cover the bottom half of Day 5 to look like water. Using colored construction paper, have the children each draw one fish and one bird. Cut them out, and affix them in the proper places.

- **Day 6: Land animals.** Using colored construction paper, have the children draw animals that live on the land. Cut them out, and affix them to the paper. Add trees and grass with tissue paper.

- **Day 7: Shabbat.** Using construction paper, have the children draw something that reminds them of Shabbat. Some ideas might include: candles (נֵרוֹת, *neirot*), *Kiddush* (קִדּוּשׁ) cup, challah (חַלָּה), Shabbat table, flowers, synagogue, resting at home. Cut them out, and affix them to the mural paper.

LESSON 3

Adam and Eve
אָדָם וְחַוָּה
Adam V'Chavah

Genesis 2:4–3:24

INTRODUCTION

In *B'reishit*, we learn that God created people on the sixth day. We now take a closer look at the first two people God created. We also learn about God's love, following and breaking rules, and the power of God's word.

In the paradise of the Garden of Eden, Adam and Eve are naked, but not initially embarrassed by their nakedness. The children are sure to giggle about this, so it is important to keep the class focused on the story. You may want to explain that Adam and Eve are naked because at this point they are like babies being cared for by God. Just as babies don't notice that they're naked, neither do Adam and Eve. When they eat the fruit of *Eitz HaDaat,* they grow up very quickly, and part of what they learn about the world is that people wear clothes.

SYNOPSIS

After God finished creating heaven and earth, God creates a man from the dust of the earth. God gives him the name Adam (אָדָם), which means "earth." God places Adam in *Gan Eden* (גַּן עֵדֶן), the Garden of Eden, filled with beautiful trees and animals. In the center of the garden stands *Eitz HaDaat* (עֵץ הַדַּעַת), the Tree of Knowledge, the tree of good and bad. God tells Adam that he may eat from any tree except *Eitz HaDaat*. Eating from the tree will cause Adam to die. God lets Adam name all of the animals but sees that Adam needs a companion. While Adam is sleeping, God takes one of Adam's ribs to create a woman to keep him company. They are naked, but they aren't embarrassed. One day the *nachash* (נָחָשׁ), the snake, walks to the woman and talks to her, convincing her that she won't die if she eats the fruit from *Eitz HaDaat*. After she eats the fruit, she also gives the fruit to Adam. Now they realize they are naked and sew fig leaves together for clothing. They hear God in the garden and hide. When they tell God they are hiding because they are naked, God realizes they have eaten from *Eitz HaDaat*. God punishes them. God takes away the legs of the *nachash* so all snakes will always have to crawl on their bellies. God tells Adam and the woman that they must leave *Gan Eden*. Adam names the woman Chavah (חַוָּה, Eve). Because God loves them, God gives Adam and Chavah clothing from animal fur to protect them. God places two cherubim with fiery swords at the gate to *Gan Eden* to guard it.

CAST

- Adam

- Woman (Chavah)

- *Nachash*

- Two cherubim

SCENERY, COSTUMES, AND PROPS

- A background with the look of a plush garden. This may include flowers, trees, and animals. One of my favorite ways to create a *Gan Eden* background is to hang a patchwork of different printed fabrics. I like to use large squares of fabric from a book of upholstery samples.

- A large tree with artificial fruit hanging for *Eitz HaDaat*. Tie or glue a string to the stem of the fruit, or find fruit-shaped ornaments that already have loops on them.

- A stuffed snake, inflatable toy, or a snake made from art materials for the *nachash*. The story starts with legs on the snake, so make legs and attach them with tape or Velcro.

- Empty rolls from wrapping paper for the flaming swords. Attach yellow, orange, and red tissue paper to one end, or glue tissue paper to the roll. (To avoid the use of toy weapons, you may choose to present these as torches.)

- Two long white T-shirts

- Two sets of clothing covered with leaves fashioned from paper, purchased from a craft store, or gathered outdoors.

- Two pinnies (see pages 9–10) of velour or fake fur

SUGGESTED SCENE AND NARRATION

Adam and Chavah are wearing long white shirts. Adam is asleep on the ground (אֲדָמָה, *adamah*) in front of *Eitz HaDaat*.

Narrator: After God finished creating heaven and earth, God creates a man from the dust of the earth. *(Adam slowly stands up.)*

God: I will give you the name Adam, which means "earth." I will place you in *Gan Eden*, the Garden of Eden. It is filled with all the beautiful trees and animals.

Narrator: Adam looks around this beautiful place and is happy.

God: Adam, you have everything you need here. You may eat from any tree you'd like **except** the fruit from *Eitz HaDaat*, the Tree of Knowledge. If you do, you will surely die.

Adam: Look at all these beautiful animals and trees. I'm going to give the animals names. Let's see . . . here's a "bear," a "cat" . . . but I would love to have a companion who could talk with me and keep me company.

Narrator: So, God puts Adam to sleep. *(Adam lays down.)* God takes one of Adam's ribs and creates a woman to be Adam's companion. *(The woman lays down next to Adam.)*

Adam *(talking to the woman as she gets up):* I'm so glad you're here. You need to know some important things. God has said that we're allowed to eat anything in this beautiful garden except the fruit from *Eitz HaDaat*. If you do, you will die.

Woman: Okay. I understand.

Narrator: One day, the woman is walking by *Eitz HaDaat* when the *nachash* walks by. *(The* nachash *with legs "walks" over.)*

Nachash: Why don't you take a bite of the fruit on *Eitz HaDaat*? Why are you afraid?

Woman: I will die if I eat that fruit.

Nachash: Nothing will happen if you take one bite!

Narrator: The woman takes a bite and nothing happens. Adam comes by.

Woman: Adam, why don't you take a bite of this piece of fruit? Nothing will happen. *(He takes a bite.)*

Adam: Look, we're naked! We need to make some clothing from leaves. *(Attach leaf clothing to their shirts.)*

Narrator: Adam and the woman hear rustling in the garden and realize God is looking for them. They hide behind the tree.

God: Adam, why are you hiding from me?

Torah Alive!

Adam and Woman: We're embarrassed because we're naked. *[Children may laugh here. Explain to them that when people are first born, they are naked.]*

God: How do you know you're naked? Did you eat the fruit from *Eitz HaDaat*?

Adam: The woman told me to eat it!

Woman: The *nachash* told me to eat it!

God: Then you will all be punished! *Nachash*, you and all snakes that come after you will no longer walk on legs. You will crawl on your bellies in the dust. *(Take off the legs from the snake.)* However, worst of all, you two must leave *Gan Eden* and never return. Since I love you, I will give you clothing from the fur of animals so you will be comfortable. *(Take off the leaves, and give them fur pinnies.)* I will put two cherubim with flaming swords at the gate of *Gan Eden* to guard it so no one will be allowed to enter again.

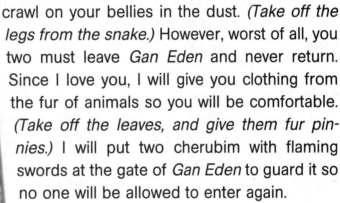

Narrator: Adam gives the woman the name Chavah. *(Position the two cherubim holding flaming swords like a bridge.)* Adam and Chavah sadly walk through the swords, out of the garden, never to return.

DISCUSSION QUESTIONS

• Why do you think Adam and Chavah disobeyed God?

• Should you listen to someone's advice without thinking about whether it's right or wrong? How can you tell when someone's advice is good or bad?

- What would you have done if you were in the garden and the snake told you to eat the fruit?

- Do you think God should have given Adam and Chavah a second chance so they could stay in *Gan Eden*?

- Why do you think God didn't give them a second chance?

PUPPETS

This will be the first time the children use their puppets (see pages 15–17). Create and add the following to the puppet bag for the children to use as props in their role-playing:

- First set of clothing for Adam and Chavah. Collect leaves from outdoors. Remove the paper from several green crayons. Cut plain white paper into 3 × 3–inch pieces. Place a leaf under the paper with the underside of the leaf touching the paper. Put pressure on the paper while rubbing with the flat side of the crayon. Make two rubbings. Cut out the leaf.

- Second set of clothing for Adam and Chavah. Cut brown velour or fur-like fabric into a 2 × 3–inch piece for each puppet.

- *Nachash.* Divide a 9 × 12–inch piece of colored construction paper or craft foam into fourths. Give each child one piece. Round the corners with scissors. Invite the children to color any design on the entire piece with markers. Starting in one corner, about ½ inch in from the edge, cut around the paper or foam in a circular pattern, moving toward the center. Leave the center a little larger to make the head of the snake. Draw two eyes on the head, or affix wiggly eyes. This will make a very long snake!

- Fruit. Draw and cut out fruit from construction paper or sheets of craft foam. You may find some small fruits in a craft store.

- Trees. Anchor empty paper towel rolls in modeling clay. Add green tissue paper for leaves. The trees probably won't fit in the puppet bag. They may be stored in the classroom.

RELATED ACTIVITIES

Individual Picture of Adam and Chavah

Collect and press small leaves between two pieces of waxed paper, and place under heavy books overnight.

Give each child two leaves. Invite them to draw a fruit tree in the center of a piece of paper. Glue the leaves on the paper. Have the children add heads, arms, and legs to the leaves and embellish the picture with all kinds of animals, plants, and flowers.

WALL TORAH

On mural paper, fashion a tree from construction or tissue paper. The children enjoy gluing crumbled tissue paper on for fruit. Fashion a *nachash*, and add it to the tree. Using many colors of construction paper, children may draw different animals, flowers, bushes, Adam, Chavah, and so on. Glue them on in collage fashion to look like *Gan Eden*.

LESSONS 4 AND 5

Noah's Ark
תֵּבַת נֹחַ
Teivat Noach

Genesis 6:9–9:17

INTRODUCTION

Long after Adam and Chavah were sent out of *Gan Eden*, there were many people in the world. The world was full of violence and destruction, and the people were behaving very badly. Among these people, God selected the most righteous man, Noach, to carry out a plan to start the world over again.

There are many exciting related activities in this unit. You could spend at least two weeks on this unit.

SYNOPSIS

God decides, because the world is so filled with evil, that it needs to be started over again. All of the people and all of the animals will be destroyed by a great flood. Only Noach (נֹחַ), his wife, their three sons—Cham (חָם), Shem (שֵׁם), and Yefet (יֶפֶת)—and their wives will be saved. (In the Torah, the wives in Noach's family are not given names. Later on, the Sages gave Noach's wife the name Naamah [נַעֲמָה].) God instructs Noach to build a great *teivah* (תֵּבָה), ark. God tells Noach to take two of every animal, a male and a female, on the *teivah*. When people see Noach and his family building the *teivah* on dry ground, they laugh at him. The animals come on the *teivah* and are given special places to live. Soon, the rain starts. As it rains, the *teivah* is lifted up by the water. The people, the houses, and the animals are all covered by the water. It rains for forty days and forty nights. Noach and his family are very busy taking care of the animals. Soon after the rain stops, Noach sends out a raven to see if the water has gone down. Then Noach sends out a *yonah* (יוֹנָה), dove. The *yonah* circles around and comes back. Noach knows the water is still too high. A week later, Noach sends the *yonah* out a second time. The *yonah* flies around and comes back with an olive branch in its mouth. From this, Noach knows the treetops are beginning to show. The third time, another week later, Noach sends out the *yonah*, and it doesn't return. Noach knows the *yonah* has found a place to build a home and it is time to let the animals off the *teivah*. After all of the animals and people are off the *teivah*, Noach thanks God for saving their lives. God sets a beautiful *keshet* (קֶשֶׁת), rainbow, in the sky. The *keshet* is a sign of God's promise that, even though there will be natural disasters, never again will there be any reason for God to destroy the entire world.

CAST

- Noach

- Noach's wife

- Noach's three sons

- The sons' three wives

- Pairs of animals

SCENERY, COSTUMES, AND PROPS

- Costumes for the animals. These may be fashioned easily by making pinnies (see pages 9–10) from animal print fabrics or felt that may be found in fabric stores, dyed or painted pillowcases, or adult-sized T-shirts that may be embellished with paint or sticky-back paper. Animal heads may be made by adding ears or antennae to old *kippot* or headbands. Party supply catalog companies sell a variety of inexpensive hats and masks with animal faces.

- Robes for Noach, his wife, their three sons, and their wives.

- A gray or white beard for Noach.

- A blank wall or surface with grass at the bottom as a backdrop for introducing the story. Cut a large *teivah* from a brown tablecloth or large piece of fabric and make horizontal lines with a permanent marker to give the effect of planks of wood.

- A white dove fashioned from paper, felt, or other materials.

SUGGESTED SCENE AND NARRATION

Narrator: A long time after Adam and Chavah, there were many people on the earth. God was very unhappy with the way people were behaving. They were very mean to each other. God decided that the people were so bad that the world needed to be destroyed and started over again. God found one man who was nicer (more righteous) than all the rest of the people. His name was Noach.

God: Noach, I am very disappointed in all of the people in the world. I will destroy everyone by sending a great flood. You are the nicest person of all. I need to save your family and two of every animal on the earth.

Noach: What should I do?

God: I will tell you how to build a *teivah*, a big ark. You and your family and the animals will be safe from the flood. Now, you need to get to work.

Narrator: Noach and his family begin to cut down trees and cut them into planks of wood. *(The children pantomime.)* They begin to hammer the planks into the shape of a *teivah*, an ark. *(Tack the* teivah *to the backdrop.)* They were building the teivah on the field near their home. When people would come by, they would laugh at Noach because he was building a boat in the middle of a field!

Noach: We need to bring the animals on the *teivah*, two by two, one male and one female. *(The animals walk over to the teivah.)*

Narrator: The wind starts to rustle the leaves on the trees. *(The children rub their hands together to make a rustling sound.)* Then the drops of rain begin to fall. *(The children snap their fingers or tap two open fingers on the opposite arm.)* The rain begins to get heavier. *(The children hit their hands, alternately, on their thighs.)* There is thunder and lightning. *(Add loud clapping.)* As the rain falls heavier and heavier, the water rises. It lifts the *teivah* up off the ground and covers all the people, all the animals, and all the houses.

Noach: How long is it going to rain? It's getting very crowded in here. Some of the animals have had babies! We have to work so hard to feed the animals and clean up!

Narrator: It rains for forty days and forty nights. Finally, the rain stops.

Noach: Look. The rain has stopped. We need to know when it will be time to open the doors and let the animals off onto dry land again. I'll send out a raven to see if there is dry land.

Narrator: Noach sends out the raven, and it flies around until the water starts to go down.

Noach: I'll send a *yonah*, a dove, this time and see what the dove finds. *(Noach holds a dove.)*

Narrator: Noach sends the dove away. The dove flies around and comes back.

Noach: It's not time to get off the *teivah*. In a few more days, I'll send the dove out again.

Narrator: A week later, Noach sends the dove out again. The dove flies away and eventually comes back. *(Attach a paper olive branch to the dove's beak.)*

Noach: Look, the dove has an olive branch in its mouth. The tops of the trees are showing. The water must be going down.

Narrator: Another week later, Noach sends the dove out one more time. A few days later, Noach realizes that the dove is not going to return.

Noach: The dove has found a place to build a home. The waters have gone down all the way. It's time to leave the *teivah* and go out onto dry land.

Narrator: Noach and his family open the doors, and the animals happily leave the *teivah*.

Noach: Thank you, God, for saving our lives. Look everyone, there's a *keshet*, a rainbow, in the sky.

God: I have sent this rainbow as a sign of my promise. I promise never to destroy the whole world again. Now you need to start the world over again and have babies and make new homes.

DISCUSSION QUESTIONS

- Why did God think it was necessary to destroy the whole world?

- How do you think God felt about this decision?

- What do you think the people were like in Noach's time? How were they behaving? How was his family different?

- Why did God save two of each animal?

- How do you think God felt after the flood?

- Why do you think a rainbow was the sign of God's promise?

- Why do you think God made a promise never to destroy the whole world again?

PUPPETS

Create the following props, and add them to the puppet bag:

- Clothing for Noach and his family. Use wallpaper or fabric scraps or other colorful paper.

- A pair of animals. Use craft foam, and attach them to craft sticks.

- A white beard for the male puppet. Cut a triangle from furry fabric or felt. Put a small piece of the stiff side of Velcro on the back of the beard so it can stick to the face of the puppet.

RELATED ACTIVITIES

Animal Pairs

Invite children to bring a stuffed animal from home, and tell them they will find the animal's pair the next day in school. Place a long, child-safe mirror on its side, on the floor. As the children place the animal in front of the mirror, the animal will see its pair (reflection).

A Special Book

Create a book for the class in the style of *Brown Bear, Brown Bear*. On the cover write, "Noah, Noah (Noach), What's on Your Ark (*Teivah*)?" On the top of each page write, "I see a pair of _____ on this ark (*teivah*)." At the bottom of the page write, "Noah, Noah (Noach), what's on your ark (*teivah*)?" Have the students illustrate a pair of animals on the page. Fill in the blank with the name of the animal.

Doves

Here's an easy way to create a dove!

Paint an old-fashioned clothespin white. Fold a round, white coffee filter to slip in the clothespin as wings for the dove. Glue a little branch or leaves to the mouth area. Hang doves from strings.

Rainbow

Create a handprint rainbow for your classroom or Wall Torah.

Cut a large semicircle of white paper. Starting on the outside of the semicircle, sketch arcs for bands of red, orange, yellow, green, blue, and purple. Estimate how many handprints it will take to complete the rainbow, and determine how many handprints each child will need to make. (Every child should be included, and each should make about the same number of handprints.) Use tempera paint to paint the children's hands, and have them make handprints on the paper to paint each color of the rainbow. Complete the rainbow with one purple handprint in the middle. As you hang your rainbow, play "The Rainbow Blessing" by Debbie Friedman, available on *Live at the Del*.

This would be a great time to teach the *b'rachah* (blessing) that is said when seeing a rainbow. Use the *b'rachah* if you're lucky enough to see one!

בָּרוּךְ אַתָּה יי אֱלֹהֵינוּ מֶלֶךְ הָעוֹלָם זוֹכֵר הַבְּרִית וְנֶאֱמָן בִּבְרִיתוֹ וְקַיָם בְּמַאֲמָרוֹ.

Baruch atah Adonai, Eloheinu Melech haolam zocheir hab'rit v'ne-eman biv'rito v'kayam b'ma-amaro.

We praise You, *Adonai* our God, Sovereign of the universe,
who remembers, is faithful to, and fulfills
Your covenant with and promise to creation.

Colors

This would be a great time to learn about colors or the Hebrew names of the colors, using the colors of the rainbow. The children can explore and experiment with finger paint, modeling clay, paints, etc. They may conduct science experiments with color mixing.

Animal Habitats

This is also a great time to discuss animal habitats. What do animals that live in cold climates need to do to get ready for winter? How do animals survive in the desert? What types of animals live in the sea?

Dances

Learn folk dances about animal pairs: "Yeish Lanu Tayish" (We Have a Billy Goat), or "HaTziporim" (Israeli Bird Dance). See Appendix A, pages 233–236, for instructions.

Children are natural dancers and are great students of animal movements. Invite them to move creatively, imitating animal movements.

Individual Murals

Invite each child to create a small mural of the Noach story using the collage technique. Starting with a large piece of blue construction paper, center and affix a brown cutout shape of a *teivah*, fashioned either by the teacher or student. Gradually add and affix the following to the collage using different art mediums:

- Noach and his wife: Use wallpaper rectangles for bodies. Children add head, arms, and legs. Use yarn or "*etrog* hair" for the hair and beard.

- Animals: Use preprinted animal skin paper or fabric cut into ovals. Children add legs, heads, and features.

- Water: Glue cut-up pieces of blue tissue paper along the bottom of the mural.

- Rainbow: Paint with watercolors or tempera.

This activity can be completed over a number of days.

Funky Animal Pairs

Create "funky" animal pairs from modeling clay. Invite the children to create a pair of original, colorful, and crazy animals. Put them on display for everyone to enjoy!

Science

In your science corner, display prisms and other color-related scientific equipment for the children to explore.

Math

In your math activities, include matching or pairs games. Animal "Memory" or "Concentration" games are lots of fun!

Special Snack

Following a recipe for rolled cookie dough (see Appendix B, page 237), bake cookies in a variety of animal shapes. Invite children to use animal-shaped cookie cutters or fashion their own original animals. Have a special *Teivat Noach* party. Yum!

WALL TORAH

The *Noach* portion of the Wall Torah can be easily made by cutting a 24 × 36–inch piece of mural paper and then affixing a brown *teivah* in the center. Invite the children to add a pair of animals. Give each child a piece of colored paper, folded in half. On one side, draw the selected

animal. Cut through both layers of paper. Illustrate the blank paper to match the first layer. Glue pairs onto the *teivah*. Children may add raindrops cut from Post-it notes so they can take them off at some point. Add water made from tissue paper below the *teivah*. When attaching this mural to the wall, place the rainbow (pages 45–46) above the picture.

LESSONS 6 AND 7

Tower of Babel
מִגְדַל בָּבֶל
Migdal Bavel

Genesis 11:1–9

INTRODUCTION

The story of *Migdal Bavel* (מִגְדַל בָּבֶל), the Tower of Babel, is actually a very short story at the end of *Parashat Noach*. However, this simple story provides an opportunity to teach about diversity, multicultural topics, family heritage, and important family values. We spend at least two weeks on this rich unit!

While the Torah does not mention King Nimrod, he is part of the midsrashic literature about this story and gives the story extra richness.

SYNOPSIS

After the great flood, Noach's family begins to increase, and eventually there are many people on the earth. They all travel together and finally find a suitable place to settle in the land of Shinar. They begin to build a town on the plain near the river. The king, Nimrod, wants his town to become a great city. He instructs the townspeople to build a great *migdal* (מִגְדָּל), tower, in the middle of the town. The people work tirelessly on the tower and begin to neglect their responsibilities to their families, livestock, and devotion to God. God sees this and confuses their language so they can no longer work together. Eventually, the people leave the *migdal* unfinished and leave their homes.

Legend tells us that people who spoke a common language traveled together and where they settled, a new country was established. For instance, people who spoke Chinese wandered and when they settled, they established the country of China. We get the word "babble," meaning "unintelligible speech," from the name of the city, *Bavel* (בָּבֶל).

CAST

- King Nimrod

- Townspeople

SCENERY, COSTUMES, AND PROPS

- This is a good time to start your collection of multicultural costumes. If you put out the word, you'll be amazed at the treasures people have in their closets or what you can find at a rummage sale!

- When teaching this lesson, you may ask the children to bring in or wear an article of clothing from a foreign country. Alternatively, you may dress up only King Nimrod and save the costumes for an international celebration at the culmination of this unit.

SUGGESTED SCENE AND NARRATION

Most children are talented architects! One way we build the *migdal* is by using large cardboard blocks, shoeboxes, or small wooden blocks. As a background, we hang posters of children from around the world.

Begin the narration with King Nimrod sitting in a chair. Pile the blocks nearby, making sure there is at least one block for each child.

Narrator: Long after the flood that destroyed all of the people except for Noach's family, there were many people in the world again. They wandered together until they found a place where they wanted to stay and build a village. They were very happy and content with their village until the king decided he wanted the village to be a great city.

King Nimrod: I want everyone to build a great *migdal*, a tower in the middle of our village so we can be a great city.

Narrator: The people agreed and began to build the great tower. *(Have a few children place their blocks to build the tower.)*

King Nimrod: Build the *migdal* higher! Make it reach the sky! *(Add more blocks.)*

Narrator: The people began to work very hard. They didn't have time to feed their children or their animals. They didn't have time to pray. *(Add more blocks.)*

King Nimrod: Work faster! We will be greater than God when our *migdal* reaches into the heavens. *(Add more blocks.)*

Narrator: God sees what is happening and realizes that the people have forgotten the really important jobs. God doesn't want to punish them. God just wants to stop them from spending all their time building the *migdal*. So God confuses their speech. Everyone begins to speak a different language, and everyone starts to fight with each other. *(Children may make believe they are arguing.)* Finally, all the people leave the *migdal*. They leave the village and build new homes in places where people speak the same language. This may explain how many of the countries around the world started. The *migdal* was never finished. It was called *Migdal Bavel,* "The Tower of Babel," because of the "babbling" speech of the people.

DISCUSSION QUESTIONS

- Why did the people build the tower?

- Why do you think King Nimrod wanted his city to be so great?

- What were some things the people forgot to do because they were so busy building the *migdal?*

- Were the people of Bavel bad?

- Why did God confuse their languages?

- What does it mean when someone "babbles"?

PUPPETS

Instead of using your Torah puppets for this unit, invite each child to create an international doll. One way is to cut body shapes from tagboard or purchase premade multicultural figures of different skin tones. Affix wiggly eyes with craft glue or hot glue. For hair, use yarn or "*etrog*" hair." Using pictures as a guide, fashion clothing for the dolls from scraps of wrapping paper or other fancy paper. If older children are available to help, this is a great activity for multi-age learning. Once the dolls are completed, add them to your classroom *migdal.*

RELATED ACTIVITIES

Multicultural Museum

Invite the children to bring in dolls, flags, or artifacts from foreign countries.

Set up two sections for the museum. One will be a "Please Touch" table labeled with a picture of two hands. The other will be a "Please Look" table for delicate items, labeled with a picture of two eyes.

Music

Play multicultural music while working or playing. (See bibliography.)

Collect and use rhythm instruments from around the world. Play music while children explore the instruments. When the music stops, the children switch instruments.

"Hello"

Learn to say "hello" in different languages. Children may interview relatives or neighbors. During circle time, they may say "hello" in another language. Here's a fun challenge! In how many languages can we count to ten?

Classroom Library

Set up a classroom library of picture books of different countries and people of different lands. (See bibliography.)

Visitors

Invite parents and friends to visit the class to share stories, songs, foods, or artifacts from foreign countries.

Folk Dances

Teach folk dances from foreign countries. (See Appendix A for instructions and music information.)

Multicultural Clothing

Young children love to "dress up"! Set up a rack of clothing, shoes, hats, jewelry, etc., from foreign countries. Try to set up a tall, child-safe mirror. The children may try on clothing and view themselves in a mirror. Take pictures!

Family Stories

Send home a questionnaire to the parents. Ask: "Where did your family go after they left Bavel?" (What countries did your ancestors come from before they came to North America?) Set up a world map, and put a pin in each country. List family names under each selected country. When lists are complete, make a bar graph and discover the ethnic background of your class.

International Festival

As a culminating activity for this unit, prepare an international festival. Invite each child to wear clothing or jewelry from another country. Serve international foods or snacks, which may be brought from home, prepared in class, or supplied by teachers. Include songs and dances from other countries. Don't forget to take pictures!

WALL TORAH

According to this story, we all have ancestors who lived in Bavel. Our families all participated in building the tower. Invite the children to tear brown paper into small rectangles to represent the bricks of the tower. Take photographs of the children, or have each child draw a picture of himself or herself and write his or her name on a piece of paper about 2 × 3 inches. After each child glues some "bricks" to the mural paper to build the tower, glue the child's picture on the bricks.

LESSON 8

Abraham and Sarah
אַבְרָהָם וְשָׂרָה
Avraham V'Sarah

Genesis 11:27–13:18

INTRODUCTION

This lesson initiates the study of the Matriarchs and Patriarchs (Mothers and Fathers) of the Jewish people. In the Torah, we first learn about Avraham (אַבְרָהָם) and Sarah (שָׂרָה) when they are already adults. The well-known story about young Avraham and the idols is a midrash, created long ago, to help us understand how Avraham may have realized there was one God. In the ancient city of Haran, Avraham lived among people who worshiped idols. The people believed that these statues of wood, stone, or metal had powers. They prayed to specific idols to fulfill their wishes.

SYNOPSIS

God says to Avraham (and Sarah), "*Lech l'cha*" (לֶךְ לְךָ), "Go!" God tells Avraham to leave his home and all the people he knows. God asks Avraham to travel to a far-off land. God promises Avraham that if he does what is asked of him, Avraham and Sarah will become the father and mother of a great nation of people. Avraham, Sarah, and their nephew Lot (לוֹט) pack their belongings, leave their home on a journey, and stop when God instructs them. They settle in the land of Canaan (כְּנַעַן). After some time, the workers who are taking care of Avraham's animals begin to argue with the workers who are taking care of Lot's animals. Avraham suggests that they each have their own land in order to end the quarreling. Lot agrees and moves his tents to the land near Sodom, while Avraham stays in the land of Canaan. Before going their own ways, they hug. God asks Avraham to look out over the land where he will stay, the land of Canaan. God promises Avraham that this land will belong to his descendants, the Jewish people, forever and that they will be like (as numerous as) the dust that covers the earth.

CAST

- Avraham

- Sarah

- Lot

SCENERY, COSTUMES, AND PROPS

- The backdrop that will become your backdrop for all of the stories that take place in Canaan (until Yoseif is sold into slavery in Egypt)

- A backdrop made from a plain bedsheet or fabric to use for the short time Avraham and Sarah are in Haran

- Robes for Avraham, Lot, and Sarah

- White beard for Avraham

- Tent

- Bags for Avraham, Lot, and Sarah (to carry their belongings)

- Music: "L'chi Lach" by Debbie Friedman (from *And You Shall Be a Blessing*, Sounds Write Productions SWP 601.)

SUGGESTED SCENE AND NARRATION

Narrator: Our great teachers tell us that Avraham came to realize that people shouldn't be praying to idols that are just carved stone or wood. They should be praying to **one** God whom we cannot see but we can feel in our hearts. The Torah tells us that one day, God speaks to Avraham.

God: Avraham, *Lech l'cha*. Leave your land and your people and go to a land far away.

Avraham: Where will I go?

God: You'll go to a place that I will tell you about. If you do what I ask of you, I will bless you. You will become the leader of a great nation of people, the Jewish people.

Avraham (turns to Sarah): Come Sarah, come, Lot, let's pack our bags and do what God asks of us. *(They make believe they are packing their bags. Play the music "L'chi Lach" as they take a slow walk around the room. As they walk, change the backdrop to Canaan. When the music is finished, they sit in front of their new home.)* Sarah and Lot, we're here in our new home in Canaan. We'll have lots of work to do here.

Narrator: Avraham and Lot are both shepherds. Soon, the people who are watching over their animals begin to fight with each other. Avraham decides they need to each have their own land so they can put an end to the fighting.

Avraham: Lot, we can't keep fighting. Why don't you choose a place where you would like to live and I'll keep my family and animals in another place.

Lot: I'd like to move away to a beautiful place that I've seen near the town of Sodom. I will be happy there. You may stay here.

Avraham: Lot, let's hug and say, "Good-bye," but promise to always remember each other.

Narrator: God spoke to Avraham and blessed him.

God: Avraham, you have been very kind. Look at the land around you. You will have many children. Just as there is so much dust on the earth that you can't count the pieces, that's how many children (descendants) you will have. I promise that this land, where you will stay, the land of Canaan, will belong to you, your children, and their children forever.

DISCUSSION QUESTIONS

- Have you ever moved? What was it like?

- If you had to leave your home, what types of things would you take with you?

- What types of things might Avraham, Sarah, and Lot have taken with them?

- Why did God ask Avraham to do something so important? *(Avraham believes in one God.)*

- Why do you think Avraham agreed to leave his home and do what God asked?

- Why do you think Avraham and Sarah are called the father and mother of the Jewish people?

- Jewish people have lived in the land of Canaan for thousands of years. Do you know the modern name for this land? *(Israel.)* What did God promise Avraham and the Jewish people?

PUPPETS

Create the following props and add them to the puppet bag:

- Clothing for Avraham, Lot, and Sarah made from wallpaper, fabric, or paper scraps.

- Sacks to carry their belongings.

- Sheep for both Avraham and Lot, which may be fashioned by affixing cotton balls to tagboard.

RELATED ACTIVITIES

What's in Your Sack?

Ask the children: "Make believe that, like Avraham and Sarah, you're leaving your home and going on a journey to another home. What would you pack in your sack?"

For each student, draw a large sack on a piece of 9 × 12–inch construction paper. Invite the children to draw several items they think would be most important to pack. Teachers or students (using inventive spelling) may write a descriptive word under each object that is drawn.

Classify and Graph

The children have "packed their sacks." Classify objects that people might bring: clothing, food, toys, Jewish objects, "security" objects. Create a bar graph with your information.

Follow the Journey

Using a map of Israel, chart the journey taken by Avraham, Sarah, and Lot.

Special Snack: Chocolate "Sacks"

1. Following the directions on a package of puff pastry, defrost and roll out sheets of dough.

2. Cut the sheets into rectangles.

3. Sprinkle with chocolate chips.

4. Roll the dough and twist the ends to form "sacks."

5. Bake according to instructions on the package of dough.

WALL TORAH

Continue adding to the Wall Torah as children draw Avraham, Sarah, and Lot carrying their bags (on their donkeys) on their journey. The background may include sun, mountains, green pastures, trees, sheep, goats, and cows.

LESSON 9

Abraham and Sarah and Their Visitors

אַבְרָהָם וְשָׂרָה וְאוֹרְחִים
Avraham V'Sarah V'Orchim

Genesis 18:1–15 and 21:1–3

INTRODUCTION

Avraham and Sarah are now quite old (almost 100!) and have become well known in Canaan for their hospitality. Their tent was open on all four sides to let people know that they could come for learning or visits at all times. Avraham and Sarah are very happy in Canaan, but they are sad because they do not have any children and know that they are too old to have any. From this story, we become aware of the importance of *hachnasat orchim* (הַכְנָסַת אוֹרְחִים), hospitality to guests.

SYNOPSIS

One very hot day, Avraham is sitting in front of his tent, while Sarah is inside. In the distance, he sees three strangers walking toward the tent. Before the strangers arrive at the tent, Avraham gets up and goes out to greet them. He asks them to sit in the shade of his tree and offers them food and drink. Sarah prepares bread, and Avraham brings it to the strangers. They ask, "Where is Sarah?" When Avraham tells them she is in the tent, they say, "We are messengers (angels) from God. Tell Sarah, even though she is very old, she will have a baby." When Avraham tells Sarah the news, she laughs! She can't believe she'll have a baby at ninety years old! Months later, she gives birth to a baby, and they name him Yitzchak (יִצְחָק) which means "he will laugh."

CAST

- Avraham

- Sarah

- Three messengers/angels

SCENERY, COSTUMES, AND PROPS

- Canaan backdrop

- Tent with four sides propped open

- A tree near the tent

- Robes for Avraham and Sarah

- White beard for Avraham

- Robes for three messengers/angels

- Food and drink on a tray

- Baby doll

SUGGESTED SCENE AND NARRATION

Narrator: One hot day, Sarah is sitting inside the tent. Avraham is sitting outside. *(The strangers are waiting in another part of the room.)*

Avraham: What a hot day! Look, Sarah, there are three strangers coming toward our tent.

Narrator: The three strangers are walking slowly toward the tent.

Avraham: I'm going to go and see if they would like to rest at our home.

Narrator: Walking quickly toward the strangers, Avraham goes to greet them.

Avraham: Would you like to sit in the shade of my tree? Please sit and I'll get you some food and drink. *(Avraham walks to the tent.)* Sarah, please fix some bread, food, and drink for our guests. *(Sarah hands Avraham a tray of food and drink.)*

Sarah: Avraham, here's some food for our guests. *(Avraham brings food to the strangers.)*

Avraham: Please have some food and drink.

Strangers (taking food): Where is your wife?

Avraham: She's in the tent.

Strangers: We are messengers from God. You and Sarah are very kind. Tell Sarah she will be having a baby.

Avraham (going to tent): Sarah, these three people are messengers from God. They said you will be having a baby!

Narrator: Sarah begins to laugh.

Sarah (laughing): I'm not going to have a baby. I'm so old!

Narrator *(gives baby doll to Sarah):* Months later, Sarah gives birth to a baby boy. They name him Yitzchak, which means "he will laugh.

DISCUSSION QUESTIONS

• Why was Avraham and Sarah's tent open on four sides? *(It was open on all four sides so people from all directions would know that they could receive Avraham and Sarah's hospitality at any time.)*

• How did Avraham and Sarah treat the guests?

• What did we learn about being kind (hospitable) to guests in our house?

• Why did God make it possible for Sarah to have a baby, even though she was really old? *(God intended for Avraham and Sarah to be the father and mother of the Jewish people and they needed a child.)*

PUPPETS

Create the following props and add them to the puppet bag:

• New clothes for the angels

• A tent made by folding construction paper or fabric to be draped over a chair

RELATED ACTIVITIES

Avraham and Sarah's Tent

Fashion a tent with four openings to remind us of Avraham and Sarah's hospitality.

1. Use one piece of 9 × 12–inch construction paper and one piece of 8½ × 11–inch copy paper.

2. Place the smaller sheet in the center of the larger sheet. In each corner, staple the white paper to the construction paper.

3. On the white paper only, cut a flap approximately 3 inches wide and 2½ inches deep in the middle of each side. Turn the flaps up. This will become Avraham and Sarah's tent.

4. Under each flap, the children may draw something that may be offered to guests to show them hospitality.

5. In the center of the paper, they may draw a picture of Avraham and Sarah.

Special Guest Chair

Children will enjoy decorating an old chair to use when special guests, *orchim,* visit the classroom. The children can give suggestions as to how the chair may be decorated. Generate a list of guests to invite for a special snack.

Special Snack: Making Bread

Children love to make and knead yeast dough. Bread or pita would be fun to make for a snack. Invite *orchim*!

WALL TORAH

Continuing the Wall Torah, invite children to draw Avraham, Sarah, three strangers, trees, sheep, food for the guests, and the sun. A tent may be fashioned from fabric or paper. Arrange the drawings, collage style, to describe this scene.

Avraham and Sarah's tent was open on 4 sides so people could always visit and learn. One hot day, Avraham greets 3 strangers and gives them shade, drink, and food. They tell Avraham they are actually angels, messengers from God. They tell him that, even though Sarah is very old, she will have a baby!

LESSON 10

The Binding of Isaac

עֲקֵדַת יִצְחָק

Akeidat Yitzchak

Genesis 22:1–19

INTRODUCTION

In this lesson, Avraham's faith in God is tested. God asks Avraham to sacrifice his son Yitzchak. When you sacrifice something, you give up something very special. In the time of the Torah, it was a common practice to make an animal sacrifice as a gift to God. God asks Avraham to do something that is very difficult.

The concepts in this story from the Torah are very sensitive and may be difficult for the young child to comprehend. Use your discretion when presenting the materials. When you do present the story, assure the children that God would never let Avraham actually kill his son.

SYNOPSIS

One day, when Yitzchak is a boy, God tests Avraham's faith. God asks Avraham to take his son Yitzchak up the mountain, build a fire, and sacrifice him as a gift to God. Early in the morning, Avraham and Yitzchak climb the mountain, carrying wood that they have gathered. When Yitzchak asks Avraham about the animal to be sacrificed, Avraham tells him God will provide the animal for the sacrifice. Avraham then places Yitzchak on a rock. As Avraham is about to sacrifice Yitzchak, an angel of God calls out, "Stop! Don't hurt your son. Now I know that you truly believe in Me." Avraham looks up and sees a ram caught in a bush. Avraham and Yitzchak sacrifice the ram, instead, as a gift to God. Because Avraham trusted in God, God blesses Avraham. God tells Avraham he will have as many descendants (the Jewish people) as there are stars in the sky and grains of sand on the ground.

CAST

- Avraham

- Yitzchak

- Ram

- Angel of God

SCENERY, COSTUMES, AND PROPS

- Canaan backdrop

- Tent

- Robes for Avraham and Yitzchak

- Belt with paper knife tucked in for Avraham

- White beard for Avraham

- Fur pinny for ram, and ram's horns attached to a *kippah* or hat

- Big rock fashioned from a table covered with cloth

- Wood for fire (wooden blocks or sticks gathered outdoors)

- Fire fashioned from crumpled yellow, orange, and red tissue paper

- Bush fashioned from a very large plant or easel covered with green cloth

SUGGESTED SCENE AND NARRATION

The scene takes place against the Canaan backdrop. The ram is hidden behind the bush.

Narrator: Avraham is sitting in front of his tent in Canaan. Yitzchak is sleeping next to the tent. Avraham hears God talking to him.

God: Avraham!

Avraham: Here I am.

God: Avraham, I would like you to take your son to the top of the mountain and sacrifice him as a gift to Me.

Avraham *(turning toward Yitzchak):* Yitzchak, we need to climb the mountain and make a sacrifice to God. Please carry this wood that I have gathered. *(Avraham and Yitzchak walk around the room, as if climbing the mountain. They stop near the big "rock.")*

Yitzchak: Father, where is the animal for the sacrifice?

Avraham: God will provide a ram for us. We'll make a fire for the sacrifice. *(Yitzchak places the wood near the "rock" and places the tissue-paper fire on top.)*

Narrator: Avraham places Yitzchak on the rock. Avraham raises his knife slowly. All of a sudden, Avraham hears an angel of God say, "Stop! Don't hurt your son. Now I know that you truly believe in Me." Avraham looks up and sees a ram caught in a bush. *(The ram crawls out from behind the bush.)* Yitzchak and Avraham put the ram on the rock, and Avraham takes out his knife to sacrifice the ram.

Angel of God: Avraham, because you have trusted so deeply in God, I will bless you. You will have as many descendants [children and grandchildren and great-grandchildren] as there are stars in the sky and sand on the ground.

Narrator: Yitzchak and Avraham go back down the mountain.

DISCUSSION QUESTIONS

• Why was God testing Avraham? (*Avraham was being tested to see if he would make a great first leader of the Jewish people. Other leaders will need to emulate him.*)

• Why did God send the ram from the bushes?

- What kind of qualities does it take to be a good leader?

- Who are the descendants of Avraham? *(The Jewish people.)*

PUPPETS

For props for their puppet scenes, have the children make rams from cotton balls glued to construction paper. Add features with markers, cut out the rams, and attach them to craft sticks.

RELATED ACTIVITIES

Family Tree

The Jewish people are the descendants of Avraham and Sarah. A pictorial representation of the "family tree" of Avraham and Sarah helps the children understand the connections. Posting it in the room will give the children opportunities to add to the tree as the year progresses. A possible configuration might be as follows:

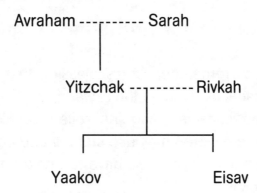

Personal Picture of God's Blessing for Avraham and Sarah

1. Construct Avraham's tent by cutting a square of fabric approximately 7 × 7 inches. Then, cut a slit up the center bottom about 4–5 inches.

Cut the two top corners off. Staple the tent to a 9 x 12-inch sheet of black construction paper, stapling the doors open.

2. Glue a picture of Avraham and Sarah, painted or drawn on a piece of paper about 2 x 3 inches, in the doorway of the tent.

3. On the top part of the black paper, affix stars.

4. On the bottom of the black paper, spread glue and pour on sand (like glitter).

Special Snack: "Star and Sand" Cookies

A yummy way to remember God's blessing that Avraham will have as many descendants as "stars in the sky and sand on the ground" is to cut out star-shaped cookies using the rolled cookie dough recipe (see Appendix B). The children may use star-shaped cookie cutters or shape the dough themselves. They will have fun decorating the stars with tiny sprinkles to look like sand.

Ram's Horn (Shofar)

The horn of the ram is used to make the shofar used by the Jewish people. Perhaps you can enlist the help of a local rabbi or parent to bring a shofar to share with the class. How is a shofar prepared? How does it sound? When do we blow the shofar? The children will enjoy trying to blow the shofar.

WALL TORAH

On the mural paper, outline a mountain. Children color or paint the mountain. Add a ram fashioned from cotton balls, Avraham, Yitzchak, bushes, sun, birds, and clouds, arranging and gluing the pictures collage style.

God tested Avraham, asking him to sacrifice his son Yitzchak. As he was about to sacrifice Yitzchak, God told Avraham to sacrifice the ram instead.

LESSON 11

Genesis 2:1–66

Eliezer Finds a Wife for Isaac

אֱלִיעֶזֶר מוֹצֵא אִשָּׁה לְיִצְחָק

Eliezer Motzei Ishah L'Yitzchak

INTRODUCTION

Avraham is now quite old, and Sarah has died. Yitzchak will become the leader of the Jewish people and needs to find a suitable wife. Yitzchak's wife will help him lead the Jewish people and will be the mother of the future leader.

It may be interesting to tell the children that in the days of the Torah, men and women had distinct roles in family life and different jobs in running the household. The Jewish people were shepherds. The fathers and sons usually took care of the herding, and the mothers and daughters took care of the home. There was no running water, so the daughters were also responsible for gathering water from the *b'eir* (בְּאֵר), the well, and bringing it home. The well was also a place where people were able to meet each other.

SYNOPSIS

Avraham asks his servant Eliezer (אֱלִיעֶזֶר) to travel to the village where Avraham used to live to find a wife for Yitzchak. Eliezer asks Avraham how he will know when he finds the right woman. Avraham assures him that one woman will stand out as having special virtues. Eliezer takes his camels and travels to the nearby village. Upon arrival, hot and tired, he goes to the well, where the women are gathered. One woman, Rivkah (רִבְקָה), not only offers Eliezer water, but offers water to his camels as well. Eliezer knows that a woman who shows kindness to animals as well as to people must be the woman who should marry Yitzchak. Eliezer gives her gifts of gold jewelry. After meeting with her family, Rivkah agrees to leave her home and return to Canaan with Eliezer. As Yitzchak is working in the field, he sees Rivkah approaching. They fall in love, and Rivkah and Yitzchak get married.

CAST

- Avraham

- Eliezer

- Yitzchak

- Rivkah

- Women at the well

- Rivkah's parents

SCENERY, COSTUMES, AND PROPS

- Canaan backdrop

- One or two tents

- A well

- A camel

- Robes for Avraham, Eliezer, Yitzchak, and Rivkah's father

- Gray or white beard for Avraham

- Long dresses for Rivkah, women at the well, and Rivkah's mother

- Several pitchers for Rivkah and women at the well

- Gold necklace and/or bracelet

SUGGESTED SCENE AND NARRATION

Narrator:	Avraham is sitting in his tent in Canaan. He calls for his servant Eliezer. Yitzchak is sitting nearby.
Avraham:	Eliezer, I'm growing very old. I need to know that Yitzchak will have a wonderful wife to help him lead the Jewish people. Please go back to where I used to live and find a wife for Yitzchak.
Eliezer:	How will I know when I find the right woman?
Avraham:	You'll see. There will be something special about her that will make her different from the other women.
Narrator:	Eliezer takes his camel and journeys to a village far away. He arrives hot and tired and goes to the well to get a drink

of water. There are several women at the well getting water for their families.

Eliezer: May I have a drink of water?

Rivkah: Of course, let me get you a drink. *(She pours water into his hands.)* Would your camels like a drink, too? *(She brings water to the camels.)*

Eliezer: You're so kind to people and animals. You are a special woman. I have been sent here to find a special wife for my master's son. Here is a gold necklace and bracelet for you as a gift from my master. May I speak to your parents to ask them if you may come with me?

Rivkah: Come, I'll take you to my home. *(Rivkah's parents can stand near another tent or another place in the room. They go to her parents.)*

Eliezer *(to her parents):* My master Avraham wishes for your daughter to marry his son Yitzchak.

Mother and Father: Rivkah, do you want to leave your home here and go with Eliezer to marry Yitzchak?

Rivkah: Yes, I do.

Mother and Father: Then you may go.

Narrator: They leave and head toward Avraham's tent. Yitzchak is standing near the tent and sees her and is happy. Rivkah sees Yitzchak and is happy.

Eliezer: Avraham, I have found a special woman who is very kind. She will be a wonderful wife for Yitzchak.

DISCUSSION QUESTIONS

- Why did Avraham feel it was so important to find a special wife for Yitzchak?

- What did Eliezer see in Rivkah that was so special? (*She was kind to both people and animals.*)

- In Jewish teachings, we are told to feed our animals before we feed ourselves. Why do you think we should do this?

PUPPETS

Create the following props, and add them to the puppet bag:

- A pitcher made from construction paper, or a small plastic cup (*Kiddush* wine/shot glass size) to be used as a prop for Rivkah. Attach it to her shoulder.

- Jewelry for Rivkah made from gold metallic paper or sequins.

- A cup to be used as a well.

RELATED ACTIVITIES

Gold Jewelry for Rivkah

You'll need:

- Empty roll from paper towels or toilet paper

- Gold foil or sticky paper

- Glitter, sequins, permanent marker, buttons, etc.

- Tacky glue

1. From an empty paper towel roll, cut a section about 1-inch wide.

2. Cut the ring open.

3. Cover the ring with foil.

4. Decorate with glitter, sequins, permanent marker, buttons, etc.

Kindness to Animals

Rivkah demonstrated the importance of caring for animals. Children are always ready to become involved in a cause for helping animals. Brainstorm with the children ways your class can help animals. List the ideas on a chart.

WALL TORAH

Your Wall Torah is growing. Now it will include a mural with a well, trees, sun, camels, Eliezer, Rivkah, other women at the well, and sheep. Arrange the pictures collage style.

As Avraham grew old, he sent his servant, Eliezer, to find a good wife for Yitzchak. At the well in another village, Eliezer chose Rivka because she showed kindness to people and animals by giving them water.

LESSON 12

The Birthright

הַבְּכוֹרָה

HaB'chorah

Genesis 25:19–34

INTRODUCTION

Eisav (עֵשָׂו) and Yaakov (יַעֲקֹב) are twins born to Rivkah and Yitzchak. They are very different. Eisav is born first. Eisav will inherit the birthright. The idea of a birthright will be a foreign concept for the children. It would be easiest to explain that, in the time of the Torah, the oldest son became the leader of the family when the father was no longer the leader. In this case, the son with the birthright will also become the next leader of the Jewish people. You might have the children who are the oldest sons in their families raise their hands. Explain that this custom is no longer practiced and, in current times, women have the same privileges and opportunities as men.

SYNOPSIS

Some time after Rivkah and Yitzchak get married, Rivkah becomes pregnant. When she is pregnant, Rivkah feels her babies moving around a lot, as if they are fighting. When Rivkah gives birth to twin baby boys, Eisav is born first. He will inherit the birthright. Eisav is covered with hair and is very noisy. Yaakov is born while holding on to Eisav's heel. Yaakov is much quieter. As the twins grow up, Eisav likes to go off hunting animals, and Yaakov enjoys staying close to home, watching the sheep, and studying about God. One day, Yaakov is cooking a pot of red lentil soup. The wonderful smell of the soup beckons Eisav as he comes back from his hunting, tired and very hungry. Eisav desperately wants a bowl of the soup. Yaakov offers to trade the soup for Eisav's birthright. Eisav agrees to the deal, giving up his right to become the future leader of the family and the Jewish people.

CAST

- Yitzchak

- Rivkah

- Eisav

- Yaakov

SCENERY, COSTUMES, AND PROPS

- Canaan backdrop

- Tent

- Toy sheep scattered around

- Long dress for Rivkah

- Robe for Yitzchak

- Two baby dolls: Eisav with red hair, Yaakov with brown or black hair

- Fur tunic and head covering for Eisav

- Toy bow and arrow for Eisav

- Long cloth tunic and head covering for Yaakov

- A fire (see page 12)

- A pot with a long spoon, on the fire

- A bowl

SUGGESTED SCENE AND NARRATION

Yitzchak (holding baby Eisav) and Rivkah (holding baby Yaakov) are sitting by their tent against the Canaan backdrop.

Yitzchak: Rivkah, how lucky we are to have twin sons. Eisav is so noisy and so big. I will enjoy hunting with him as he grows up. Eisav will inherit the birthright because he was born first.

Rivkah: Yaakov is much more quiet and very gentle. He will enjoy taking care of the sheep and staying close to home.

(Remove the tent. The next scene begins with Yaakov against the backdrop, surrounded by sheep, cooking the lentil soup over the fire. Eisav is off in another part of the scene (room) hunting. Eisav approaches Yaakov looking very tired.)

Eisav: Yaakov, I'm so hungry. I really want a bowl of that wonderful smelling red lentil soup.

Yaakov: Would you give me your birthright in exchange for a bowl of this lentil soup?

Eisav: Sure, you can have the birthright. All I want right now is a bowl of that wonderful lentil soup.

Yaakov: Okay, Eisav. Remember, when our father is no longer leader, I will be the leader of the family and the Jewish people, not you.

(Eisav gobbles the soup and goes on his way, leaving Yaakov by the fire.)

DISCUSSION QUESTIONS

- How were Yaakov and Eisav different?

- What was different about their relationships with their parents?

- Why do you think Eisav gave up his birthright for a bowl of soup? Was it for reasons other than just being hungry? *(Perhaps he really didn't care if he became the leader of the Jewish people.)* What would you have done?

- What is something that is very important to you? What would convince you to give it up?

PUPPETS

Create the following props, and add them to the puppet bag:

- Rectangular piece of fur fabric for Eisav

- Rectangular piece of cloth or wallpaper for Yaakov

- A small amount of red lentils wrapped in plastic wrap or glued to a piece of paper

RELATED ACTIVITIES

Picture of Yaakov and Eisav

Guide the children by reviewing the number of people in the scene. Discuss what else they saw in the scene (fire, pot, sheep, sun, palm trees, sand dunes).

You'll need for each child:

- A piece of 9 × 12–inch construction paper

- A piece of fur, about 2 × 3 inches

- A piece of cloth, about 2 × 3 inches

- Lentils (red if possible)

- Markers

- Tissue paper (fire colors)

1. Invite children to glue the fur and cloth on the construction paper. Add features for Yaakov and Eisav with markers.
2. Using tissue paper, fashion a fire.
3. Draw a pot on the fire. Glue dried red lentils in the pot.
4. Draw a background. This may include palm trees, hills with sheep, sky, birds, etc.

Lentil Soup

There's a wonderful sensory opportunity when simmering lentil soup in your room. Here's a recipe to try for snack or lunch. Try to cook it in your room so the children can appreciate its wonderfully enticing aroma.

Lentil Soup

1 lb. of dried lentils, rinsed and drained

1 medium onion, chopped

28 oz. can of plum tomatoes with liquid

1 c. shredded carrots (optional)

1 c. chopped celery (optional)

8 c. of water

2 bay leaves

2 tsp. salt

½ tsp. pepper

Optional: herbs such as basil or oregano

Bring all ingredients to a boil in a large pot. Simmer until tender, about 3–4 hours. Remove bay leaves. Spoon the soup into cups or bowls. Enjoy!

Family Tree

Add Yaakov and Eisav to your class family tree.

WALL TORAH

Add to your expanding Wall Torah collages a mural with a fire, a pot with lentils, Eisav in furry clothing, Yaakov in cloth clothing, grazing sheep, mountains, sand dunes, and the sun.

Ya'akov and Rivka have twin sons. As they grow up, Esau, the hunter, trades his birthright for a bowl of Ya'akov's lentil soup.

LESSON 13

Isaac Blesses His Sons

יִצְחָק מְבָרֵךְ אֶת בָּנָיו

Yitzchak M'vareich et Banav

Genesis 27:1–28:9

INTRODUCTION

This portion from the Torah deals with very delicate issues. Not only do we deal with sibling rivalry, but also we experience a parent's apparent preference of one child over the other. On the surface, it appears that Rivkah shows favoritism toward Yaakov. With a deeper look, we see that Rivkah was concerned with the future of the Jewish people and made a very difficult decision to ensure the strong leadership of the Jewish people.

SYNOPSIS

Yitzchak is growing very old, is nearly blind, and feels as though he may not live much longer. He wants to bless his oldest son, who will take over as leader of the Jewish people. Rivkah hears Yitzchak tell Eisav to hunt for an animal and make the stew they enjoy eating, and that upon his return, Yitzchak would give him the blessing. Rivkah realizes that Eisav will not make a good leader of the Jewish people. Eisav does not love God the way Yaakov does. Rivkah tells Yaakov to trick his father and receive the blessing instead of Eisav. Yaakov reminds his mother that Eisav is hairy, while his own skin is smooth. Rivkah prepares the food and covers Yaakov's smooth arms with fur from an animal. Yaakov brings the stew to Yitzchak. Yitzchak questions Yaakov because his voice doesn't sound like Eisav's. As Yaakov comes closer, Yitzchak touches his "hairy" arms and is convinced that Yaakov is actually Eisav. Yitzchak gives Yaakov the blessing of the first son, and Yaakov leaves. Soon after, Eisav returns with his stew, only to find out that Yaakov has tricked Yitzchak, and Eisav can no longer receive the blessing. Rivkah learns that Eisav has vowed that upon the death of his father, Yitzchak, he will kill his brother, Yaakov. Fearing for Yaakov's life, Rivkah tells Yaakov to run away to the home of her brother Lavan (לָבָן) for safety.

CAST

- Yitzchak

- Rivkah

- Eisav

- Yaakov

SCENERY, COSTUMES, AND PROPS

- Canaan backdrop

- Tree

- Tent with chair in front

- Fur clothing for Eisav

- Bow for hunting for Eisav

- Cloth robe for Yaakov

- Fur strips for Yaakov's arms

- Long dress for Rivkah

- Robe for Yitzchak

- White or gray beard for Yitzchak

- Two bowls

- Sheep

SUGGESTED SCENE AND NARRATION

Yitzchak sits outside his tent, against the Canaan background.

Narrator: Yitzchak is old and blind. He feels that soon he will die. He wants to give blessings to his sons. As Yitzchak calls to his son, Eisav, Rivkah is nearby, behind a tree, listening to Yitzchak.

Yitzchak: Eisav, please come here. I would like to give you the special blessing of the oldest son. *(Eisav walks over to Yitzchak.)*

Please go hunt for an animal, make the stew that we often enjoy eating, bring it to me to eat, and then I will give you the blessing.

Eisav: OK, father. I will go hunting now and I will return later. *(Eisav goes away.)*

Rivkah *(by the tree)*: Yaakov, your father is ready to give Eisav the blessing of the first son. Eisav will not be a good leader of the Jewish people. He doesn't love God and pray to God. You love God. You will make a better leader of the Jewish people. You need to trick your father and receive the blessing instead of Eisav.

Yaakov: Mother, as soon as my father touches my smooth skin, he will know that I am not Eisav.

Rivkah: Here, you will put the fur of an animal on your arms. When your father touches your arms, he will think you are Eisav. *(Rivkah puts fur strips on Yaakov's arms.)* Now, take this stew, give it to your father, and receive his blessing. *(Yaakov takes the stew and goes to Yitzchak's tent.)*

Yaakov: Father, I've brought you the stew you like, and I'm ready to receive your blessing.

Yitzchak: Come closer my son. Let me touch your arms. You have the voice of Yaakov *(Yitzchak, with "blind" eyes, reaches for "Eisav's" arms)*, but you have the arms of Eisav. Yes, I can tell now that you are Eisav. Let me touch your head and give you the blessing of the oldest son. *(Yaakov bows his head as Yitzchak reaches to bless him.)* When I am gone, you will be the leader of the Jewish people. *(Yaakov goes back to his mother, Rivkah.)*

Narrator: A few minutes later, Eisav returns with the stew he made.

Eisav *(returning with a bowl of stew)*: Father, here is your stew. I'm ready for the blessing.

Yitzchak: I already gave you the blessing!

Eisav: You didn't give me the blessing, father!

Yitzchak: Oh no, your brother, Yaakov, tricked me, and I already gave him the special blessing of the first son. I can't give you that blessing now. Now I can only give you a regular blessing.

Eisav *(walking away from the tent; Rivkah is listening from behind the tree):* When our father is no longer here, I will kill my brother, Yaakov!

Rivkah: Yaakov, you need to run away to the village of my brother, Lavan. There, you will be safe from Eisav's anger. *(Yaakov runs away.)*

DISCUSSION QUESTIONS

• Why did Yitzchak want to bless his sons?

• Why did Rivkah help to trick Yitzchak? Do you think she did the right thing?

• How do you think Yaakov felt?

• Why is Eisav angry?

PUPPETS

Create the following props, and add them to the puppet bag:

• A strip of fur or fur-like fabric for Yaakov's arms

• A white beard for Yitzchak

RELATED ACTIVITIES

Yaakov Makes Believe He Is Eisav

You'll need:

- Templates for puppets

- Tagboard or heavy paper

- Craft sticks

- Cloth fabric or wallpaper

- Fur fabric

- Velcro or paper clips

1. Trace the template for the puppets onto tagboard or heavy paper, and cut one for each child. Attach a craft stick to the back.

2. Cut out circles from the tagboard for faces. Cut out feet and hands. Children will affix and embellish the head. Affix the hands and feet.

3. Trace the templates for the biblical robes onto wallpaper or other patterned paper and cut out. Children may choose clothing to glue onto the body. Cut small pieces of fur. Attach to the arms with self adhesive Velcro or paper clips.

4. Take off fur when puppet is Yaakov. Attach fur when puppet is Eisav look-alike.

Sensory Discrimination

In this lesson Yitzchak is blind. He came to the conclusion that Yaakov was Eisav by touching Yaakov, without seeing him. The children will love to experiment with this concept. Take turns blindfolding a child and see if he or she can identify classmates by touching them or listening to their voices.

Experiment with exploring objects of different textures in a large box, with two holes cut out for the chidren's hands. The children will have fun trying to identify a variety of objects. Stretch their imagination!

WALL TORAH

Invite the children to fashion mountains, sand dunes, Eisav dressed in a fur tunic hunting for an animal, Rivkah behind a tree, Yitzchak sitting outside his tent, Yaakov with fur on his arms standing in front of Yitzchak, and the sun.

Ya'akov tricks Yitzchak and receives the blessing of the first son.

LESSON 14

Jacob's Ladder
סֻלָם יַעֲקֹב
Sulam Yaakov

Genesis 28:10–22

INTRODUCTION

Yaakov has a dream about angels on a *sulam* (סֻלָם), ladder. Later in his life, Yaakov will have another experience with an angel.

SYNOPSIS

Yaakov is running away from home and his brother, Eisav. As night approaches, he becomes tired and decides to sleep by the side of the road. He takes a large rock to use as a pillow. After he falls asleep, he has a dream. There is a *sulam* from the ground up to heaven. Angels, *malachim* (מַלְאָכִים), are going up and down the ladder. God is standing at the top of the ladder. God tells Yaakov that the land will belong to him and his family forever. God also tells Yaakov that his family will grow to be very large and all the families of the earth will be blessed by his family. God assures Yaakov that he should not be afraid or lonely because God will always be with him, protect him, and bring him back to his home. When Yaakov wakes up, he says, "God was here and I didn't know it." Yaakov no longer feels afraid or lonely and realizes that this is a very special place. He calls the place *Beit El* (בֵּית אֵל), House of God. He places his rock by the side of the road as a sign to other travelers of God's goodness.

CAST AND CREW

- Yaakov

- Angels

- Lighting director

SCENERY, COSTUMES, AND PROPS

- Canaan backdrop

- "A-frame" construction or ladder

- Small pillow that looks like a rock

- Robe for Yaakov

- Brightly colored robes for angels

SUGGESTED SCENE AND NARRATION

Yaakov stands in front of the desert backdrop.

Narrator: Yaakov is walking and walking as he leaves his home to get away from his brother Eisav. He is becoming quite tired.

Yaakov: Oh, I'm getting so tired. I think I'll rest on the side of the road. I'll take one of these rocks to use as a pillow. *(Yaakov places a pillow on the floor and goes to sleep. Make the room darker.)*

Narrator: Yaakov falls into a much needed sleep.

(As Yaakov sleeps, put the A-frame ladder in the scene. Several angels will stand on the ladder at varying heights. Turn a light on above the ladder.)

Yaakov *(rubbing his eyes):* Look at these beautiful *malachim*, these angels!

God: Yaakov, don't be afraid. Don't feel lonely. I will always be with you. This land will be yours forever. You will have a very large family. I will always protect you and bring you back to your home.

(Yaakov goes back to sleep. Take away the ladder and angels. Turn on all the lights.)

Yaakov: This dream was a sign from God. I don't feel scared anymore. I don't feel lonely anymore. God has promised to always be with me. This is a wonderful place. I'm going to call it *Beit El*, House of God. I'll take the rock that I used as a pillow and put it by the side of the road. People who pass by will know it's a sign that God is wonderful and great!

Narrator: Yaakov places the rock by the side of the road *(prop the pillow against the backdrop)* and continues on his journey to his uncle's village.

DISCUSSION QUESTIONS

- Why was Yaakov running away?

- Why do you think it was important for God to let Yaakov know that God would be with him? *(It may have given him courage to go on.)*

- What similarities do you see between God's promise to Avraham and God's promise to Yaakov? *(The land will always belong to them.)*

- Using rocks to mark special places was very common in biblical times. Do we do anything like that now? Can you think of any examples? *(Monuments, gravestones)*

PUPPETS

Create the following props, and add them to the puppet bag:

- New clothes for the angels.

- A piece of gold tinsel or metallic/glittery paper to put behind the angels' heads.

- A small ladder cut from construction paper for each child. (When you take apart old miniblinds, the string holding them together looks like a ladder. Give each child a piece of the string.)

RELATED ACTIVITIES

Jacob's Ladder

You'll need:

- Copy paper

- Scissors

- Pencil and ruler

- Construction paper

- Markers

- Stapler

1. Fold a piece of 4¼ × 11–inch copy paper in half on the long side. The folded paper will measure 11 × 2⅛ inches.

2. Draw horizontal lines from the folded side, 1½ inches in length and 2 inches apart.

3. On the non-folded side, draw the same lines, in between the first lines.

4. Open the paper, and photocopy it onto paper of your choice.

5. Give the children the folded and trimmed papers, and instruct them to cut on the lines **only**!

6. When you open up the cut paper and stretch it out, it will look like a ladder.

7. Staple the ladder to heavy paper.

8. On separate paper, fashion and cut out Yaakov and several angels.

9. Affix the angels to the ladder.

Dream Pillow

Yaakov used a rock as a pillow while he had his wonderful dream. God was with him during his dream, and he felt wonderful knowing this. Children will fashion a "dream pillow," decorated with a design that gives them the wonderful feeling that God is with them as they sleep and dream.

You'll need:

- Two squares of fabric, approximately 12 × 12 inches

- Copy paper

- Fabric crayons

- An iron

- Batting to stuff the pillow

- Tacky glue

1. Invite the children to generate ideas of things that make them "feel" God's presence (e.g., a rainbow, flowers, family, Shabbat).

2. On copy paper, using fabric crayons, have the children illustrate their ideas. (As an alternative to fabric crayons, you may use another technique directly on the fabric, such as tie-dyeing, liquid watercolors, or food coloring.)

3. Using the iron, transfer the design to the fabric.

4. On three sides, glue (or sew) the two pieces of fabric together.

5. Stuff the pillow with batting.

6. Secure the fourth side.

7. The pillow may be used in school during rest time or sent home.

WALL TORAH

Cover all but the bottom 2 inches of the mural paper with black paper. Cut out a ladder and attach it to the mural. Invite children to fashion Yaakov sleeping on a rock, angels going up and down the ladder, and shining stars.

As Ya'akov runs away, he gets tired and goes to sleep on a rock. He dreams of angels going up and down a ladder. When he wakes up, he knows God will always be with him.

LESSON 15

Jacob Meets Rachel
יַעֲקֹב וְרָחֵל
Yaakov V'Racheil

Genesis 29:1–20

INTRODUCTION

Once again, we experience the *b'eir* (בְּאֵר), the well, as a critical meeting place for personalities of the Torah. The Jewish people of the Torah were shepherds and shepherdesses. Watering the sheep was a very important job. Later in the Torah, we learn how Yaakov becomes very wealthy because of his expertise in raising sheep.

SYNOPSIS

Yaakov finally reaches the village of his Uncle Lavan. As he enters the village, he sees the well with a large rock on top. Sheep are gathered by the well. Yaakov asks two men by the well if they know his Uncle Lavan. They answer, "Yes, and here comes his daughter Racheil (רָחֵל) getting ready to water her sheep." Yaakov lifts the heavy rock from the well and helps Racheil water her flock. He kisses her hand. Racheil is surprised, but Yaakov tells her that he is Rivkah's son (her cousin). Racheil brings him to her home, and Lavan greets him warmly. Yaakov meets Racheil's older sister, Lei-ah (לֵאָה). Lavan invites him to stay, and Yaakov works for him as a shepherd. Yaakov falls in love with Racheil. Lavan offers to pay Yaakov. Yaakov asks that he be able to marry Racheil instead of receiving money for his work. Lavan agrees, and Yaakov works seven years in order to marry Racheil.

CAST

- Racheil

- Yaakov

- Lavan

- Lei-ah

- Two shepherds

SCENERY, COSTUMES, AND PROPS

- Canaan backdrop

- A well with large rock (box) on top

- Sheep around the well

- Long dresses for Racheil and Lei-ah

- Pitcher for Racheil

- Robes for Yaakov, Lavan, and shepherds

- Tent (off to the side)

SUGGESTED SCENE AND NARRATION

Place the rock-covered well in front of the Canaan backdrop. Place the sheep near the well.

Narrator: As Yaakov approaches his uncle's village, two shepherds are standing near the well. Yaakov is walking toward the well.

Yaakov: Good day, men. I'm looking for my Uncle Lavan. Do you know him?

Shepherds: Yes, we do. And here comes his daughter Racheil, getting ready to water her flock.

Narrator: Racheil is walking toward the well with her pitcher.

Yaakov: Please, let me lift off this heavy rock for you so you can get some water for your sheep.

Narrator: Yaakov lifts the heavy rock and drops it on the ground. Yaakov takes Racheil's hand and kisses it. Racheil giggles!

Racheil: Who are you? I've never seen you before.

Yaakov: I'm Yaakov, the son of Rivkah, your father's sister. I'm your cousin.

Racheil: You must come to my home and meet my father, Lavan.

Narrator: Racheil brings him to her father's tent. Lei-ah and Lavan are by the tent.

Racheil: Father, Lei-ah, this is Yaakov. He is the son of Rivkah.

Narrator: After Yaakov has stayed with Lavan's family for a few weeks, Lavan invites Yaakov to live with them. In the meantime, Yaakov has fallen in love with Racheil.

Lavan: Yaakov, you must come live with us. You may stay here and work on my land. How much should I pay you?

Yaakov: I don't want you to pay me. Instead of money, I would like to marry your daughter Racheil.

Lavan: That's fine. After working for me for seven years, you may marry Racheil.

DISCUSSION QUESTIONS

• Why do you think Yaakov fell in love with Racheil so quickly?

• What was the arrangement Lavan made with Yaakov?

- Do you think the deal Lavan made with Yaakov was fair?

- Seven years is a long time. Can you think of anything for which you would work so hard?

PUPPETS

Add to the puppet bag new clothes, fashioned from fabric, wallpaper, or construction paper, for Racheil, Lei-ah, and Lavan.

RELATED ACTIVITIES

Create a Well with Sheep

You'll need:

- A paper or plastic cup, about 7–9 ounces.

- Gray and white construction paper

- Cotton balls or batting

- Markers

1. Cut a strip of gray construction paper to fit around the cup.

2. Draw rocks on the paper, and wrap it around the cup. Glue or staple the paper closed.

3. Make sheep by gluing cotton balls to paper. Add details such as the sheep's head, legs, and tail. Cut out the sheep.

4. Place a piece of crumpled paper on top of the well to look like a rock. Children may use these props with the puppets or create another scene.

WALL TORAH

Have the children illustrate or construct a well with a rock on top, Yaakov, Racheil, sheep, trees, and mountains or sand dunes. Arrange the artwork in collage style.

LESSON 16

Jacob, Rachel, and Leah
יַעֲקֹב, רָחֵל, וְלֵאָה
Yaakov, Racheil, V'Lei-ah

Genesis 29:21–30

INTRODUCTION

What goes around comes around! Yaakov, who has been involved in deceiving both his brother and his father, is now tricked by his uncle/father-in-law, Lavan.

Lei-ah, Racheil's older sister, is often portrayed as being less physically attractive than Racheil. It is important that the children understand, however, that people should not be judged strictly on their looks and that people have many qualities that make them attractive. Additionally, it will be important for the children to know that in the time of the Torah, men could have more than one wife, and that marrying one's first cousin was common.

SYNOPSIS

After dutifully working for Lavan for seven years, Yaakov is now ready to marry Racheil. Lavan arranges a wedding and, unbeknownst to Yaakov, brings Lei-ah, covered in a heavy veil. In the morning, after the marriage, when it is light out, Yaakov lifts her veil and realizes he has been tricked into marrying Lei-ah. Angry at Lavan, Yaakov still wants to marry Racheil. Lavan agrees that he can also marry Racheil, but he will have to work for Lavan for another seven years. Yaakov's love for Racheil is so strong that he agrees to the deal. In the meantime, Yaakov learns to love Lei-ah and has several children with her. In all, Yaakov has twelve sons and one daughter.

CAST

- Yaakov

- Lavan

- Lei-ah

- Racheil

- Wedding guests

SCENERY, COSTUMES, AND PROPS

- Canaan backdrop

- Robes for Yaakov, Lavan, Lei-ah, and Racheil

- A veil made from an old tablecloth or window curtains

- Robes for wedding guests

SUGGESTED SCENE AND NARRATION

With the Canaan scene in the background, Yaakov pantomimes working. Lavan comes to Yaakov.

Yaakov: Lavan, I have been working for you for seven years without earning any money. We agreed that I could marry Racheil when I finished my work for you. I'm ready to get married now.

Lavan: You're right, Yaakov. I'll arrange a wedding and bring your bride.

Narrator: In the evening, Lavan leaves and gets Yaakov's bride. He comes back with Lei-ah covered in a heavy veil. Several guests come, too.

Lavan: Yaakov, you may take your bride home now.

Narrator: Yaakov and his bride walk away to go home. In the morning, Yaakov lifts her veil and screams in surprise.

Yaakov: You're not Racheil! You're Lei-ah!

Narrator: Yaakov angrily goes to Lavan.

Yaakov: Lavan, you tricked me! I was supposed to marry Racheil. Instead, you tricked me into marrying Lei-ah! Why did you do that?

Lavan: Yaakov, Lei-ah is older, so she should be married first.

Yaakov: But I still love Racheil!

Lavan: You may still marry Racheil, but you need to work for me for another seven years!

Yaakov: I love Racheil so much that I will work for you another seven years without getting paid.

Narrator: Another seven years went by while Yaakov worked hard. *(Yaakov pantomimes working.)* Yaakov lived happily with his wives and eventually became the father of twelve sons and one daughter.

DISCUSSION QUESTIONS

- Why was Yaakov willing to work fourteen years to marry Racheil? *(He loved her very deeply.)*

- What do you think of Lavan tricking Yaakov?

- Yaakov was tricked into marrying Lei-ah. Can you think of any other "tricks" that happened in Yaakov's life? *(He tricked his father, Yitzchak, and received the blessing of the first son.)*

PUPPETS

To the puppet bag, add a veil cut from a rectangle of lace or other fabric about 4 × 2 inches. Use it for Lei-ah and Racheil.

RELATED ACTIVITIES

Reversible Racheil/Lei-ah Doll

You'll need:

- Puppet templates

- Tagboard

- Tongue depressor or craft stick

- Cloth for veil and dresses

- Yarn for hair

- Markers

- Scissors

1. Cut two female puppet templates for each child.

2. Trace the female puppet templates onto wallpaper or other paper.

3. Give each child two bodies, two dresses, two faces, one veil, and a tongue depressor or craft stick.

4. Place the bodies and faces back to back.

5. Before stapling together, place the tongue depressor or craft stick in between the bodies, sticking out at the bottom as a holder.

6. Place the veil in between the top of the heads.

7. Staple the two dolls together.

8. Embellish the dolls with details like hair, hands, and feet.

9. As the doll is turned around, place the veil over one doll's face.

Family Tree

Add Racheil and Lei-ah to the family tree.

WALL TORAH

Fashion pictures of Yaakov, Racheil, and Lei-ah, in wedding clothes. Invite the children to decorate and arrange the picture in desert wedding style!

LESSON 17

Jacob Becomes Israel

יַעֲקֹב נֶהֱיָה לְיִשְׂרָאֵל

Yaakov Neheyah L'Yisrael

Genesis 32:4–33

INTRODUCTION

Yaakov has been away from his home for twenty years. Lavan has given Yaakov a lot of his own sheep, and Yaakov has become a very successful and wealthy shepherd. God tells Yaakov to return to his homeland, but Yaakov knows that he needs to pass Eisav's camp along the way. He is afraid that his family may be harmed and is trying to make good decisions for the welfare of his family. On his journey, he prepares gifts to give to Eisav to appease Eisav's anger.* Yaakov brings his family to a safe place and sets up his own camp to be by himself.

*This lesson may be easily connected to the next lesson, "Esau Forgives Jacob."

SYNOPSIS

Yaakov is at his tent alone. He is very troubled about the safety of his family and cannot sleep. He gets up and paces in front of his tent. Suddenly, Yaakov is grabbed from behind by a stranger. He wrestles with the stranger all night, until the morning. During their struggle, Yaakov's hip is injured. Finally, Yaakov throws the stranger to the ground and holds him down. Yaakov realizes that the stranger is an angel from God. The angel asks Yaakov to let go. Yaakov says, "I won't let go until you give me a blessing." The angel answers, "You will no longer be called Yaakov; your name will now be Yisrael (יִשְׂרָאֵל), Israel, which means, 'One who can wrestle with God.'"

CAST AND CREW

- Yaakov

- Stranger/angel

- Lighting director

SCENERY, COSTUMES, AND PROPS

- Canaan backdrop

- Yaakov's tent

- Robes for Yaakov and the stranger/angel

SUGGESTED SCENE AND NARRATION

Against the Canaan desert backdrop, Yaakov is sitting by his tent at night. *(Darken the room.)*

Narrator: God has told Yaakov to take his family back to his home-land, away from Lavan's land. Yaakov gathers his family and animals and begins on his journey. One night, while his family sets up camp, Yaakov decides to camp alone.

Yaakov: I'm so worried that my family may be in danger because we are going back home and need to pass by the camp of Eisav. Eisav is probably still angry with me for stealing his birthright. He might kill my family and me. I will send him presents and also pray to God to help me. I don't know what else to do!

Narrator: Suddenly, Yaakov is grabbed from behind by someone. They begin to wrestle.

Yaakov: What is this? Who is this wrestling with me?

Narrator: Yaakov and the stranger wrestle all night long. The stranger wrestles so hard that he twists Yaakov's hip, and Yaakov is in great pain. Yaakov holds on and finally throws the stranger on the ground. *(Turn the lights on.)*

Yaakov: Finally, it's morning! Who are you?

Stranger: Let me go!

Yaakov: Not unless you give me a blessing!

Stranger: What is your name?

Yaakov: My name is Yaakov.

Stranger: Your name will not be Yaakov anymore. Your name will now be *Yisrael. Yisrael* means "you have wrestled with God."

Narrator: Yaakov realizes the stranger must be an angel from God. The stranger leaves and Yaakov goes on his way, limping on his hurt hip.

DISCUSSION QUESTIONS

- Why was Yaakov wrestling with the stranger? Do you think Yaakov was wrestling with something or someone else? (*Perhaps Yaakov was wrestling with God. Perhaps he was wrestling with the deeds of his past.*)

- Was this Yaakov's first experience with an angel?

- What was troubling Yaakov? (*Perhaps he was worried about his family or about meeting Eisav.*)

- How do you think Yaakov felt after the wrestling match?

PUPPETS

Use the angel clothing from previous lessons.

RELATED ACTIVITIES

Yisrael Pictures

Yaakov's new name, Yisrael (Israel in English) is very important. All Jews are descendants of Yaakov or Yisrael. That is why the Jewish people are called *B'nei Yisrael* (בְּנֵי יִשְׂרָאֵל), the Children of Israel, or *Am Yisrael* (עַם יִשְׂרָאֵל), the people of Israel. The homeland of the Jewish people is called *Eretz Yisrael* (אֶרֶץ יִשְׂרָאֵל), the Land of Israel, and when the Jewish people created their state, they called it *M'dinat Yisrael* (מְדִינַת יִשְׂרָאֵל), the State of Israel.

This activity will help the children understand the connection between Yaakov/Yisrael and *Eretz Yisrael.*

You'll need:

- Blue construction paper, 9 × 12 inches

- A small Israeli flag, approximately 6 × 8 inches

- Markers

- Scissors

- Glue

1. Hold the construction paper vertically. Glue the small flag to the top half of the paper.

2. On another piece of paper, invite the children to draw Yaakov/Yisrael wrestling with the stranger. Attach this picture beneath the flag.

WALL TORAH

Cover all but the bottom 2 inches of the mural paper with black paper. Invite the children to fashion a tent from fabric or paper. Draw and cut out a figure of Yaakov wrestling with the stranger. Draw and cut out stars from metallic paper, or use prepared stars.

Ya'akov wrestles with an angel and his name is changed to "Yisrael."

LESSON 18

Esau Forgives Jacob
סְלִיחָה
S'lichah

Genesis 32:4–33:17

INTRODUCTION

Yaakov has been away from his home for twenty years. It is time to return home with his large family. He is scared to see his brother after all these years. This Torah story provides us with a wonderful opportunity to talk about forgiveness, especially among family members.

SYNOPSIS

Yaakov sends his servants ahead to see Eisav's camp. They report back that he has many soldiers. Yaakov is worried that Eisav is still angry with him for receiving the blessing of the first son. Yaakov sends his servants back to Eisav with gifts of animals, hoping it will make Eisav happy. The time finally comes for Yaakov to bring his family past the camp of Eisav. When Yaakov reaches Eisav, Eisav throws his arms around Yaakov and hugs and kisses him. They cry in each other's arms. Eisav is happy to meet Yaakov's family. Eisav forgives Yaakov. He tells Yaakov to pass by in peace with his family and hopes they both have successful lives.

CAST

- Yaakov

- Eisav

- Racheil

- Lei-ah

- Yaakov's servants (two or more)

- Eisav's soldiers

- Family members of Yaakov and Eisav

SCENERY, COSTUMES, AND PROPS

- Canaan backdrop

- Yaakov's tent

- Furry tunics for Eisav and his soldiers

- Hunting bow for Eisav

- Spears made from yardsticks or empty wrapping paper rolls for Eisav's soldiers

- Robes for Yaakov and servants

- Two sheep

- Long dresses for Racheil and Lei-ah

SUGGESTED SCENE AND NARRATION

Yaakov is at his tent with two of his servants. In another part of the room, Eisav is at his camp with his soldiers and family.

Narrator: Yaakov is getting ready to bring his family home to the place in Canaan where he grew up.

Yaakov (to his servants): Please go ahead and see where Eisav lives. Report back to me about Eisav's camp.

Narrator: His servants leave and walk toward Eisav's camp.

Servants *(returning to Yaakov):* Yaakov, Eisav has many soldiers at his camp!

Yaakov: I will send him some gifts of my finest animals. Please bring him these sheep and tell him they are a gift from me.

Narrator: Yaakov gives the servants two sheep.

Yaakov: Maybe he will let me pass by his camp without hurting me and my family. *(The servants take the sheep to Eisav.)*

Servants *(to Eisav):* These sheep are from my master, Yaakov. He would like you to have them as a gift.

Narrator: A few days later, Yaakov gathers his family together to begin their journey. His wives walk next to him. His children follow.

Yaakov: Come, my family. It's time to go back home. I want to return to the land where I grew up. I hope we will be safe as we pass by my brother Eisav's camp.

(Yaakov walks slowly toward Eisav's camp.)

Narrator: The two brothers walk slowly toward each other. Eisav carries the sheep Yaakov had sent him.

Eisav *(putting the sheep on the ground and opening his arms wide):* My brother, Yaakov, I don't need your gifts. I only want your love. *(Eisav gives Yaakov a big hug!)*

Narrator: Eisav and Yaakov hug and kiss each other and begin to cry.

Yaakov: You're not angry with me anymore for tricking you?

Eisav: Yaakov, I know you'll be a great leader. I don't want to be a leader of the Jewish people. Of course, I forgive you. Who are all these people?

Yaakov: These are my wives and children. We're returning to our homeland.

Eisav: Would you like some help?

Yaakov: Thank you, but we're fine.

Eisav:	Please, continue on your journey. I hope you have happiness and peace in your lives.
Narrator:	Yaakov and his family continue past Eisav on their journey home.

DISCUSSION QUESTIONS

- Why was Yaakov scared? (*He thought Eisav might kill him and his family.*)

- Why do you think Eisav was so happy to see Yaakov and forgive him?

- Do you think Eisav should have forgiven Yaakov?

- Why do you think that Yaakov refused Eisav's help?

PUPPETS

No new props are necessary for this lesson.

RELATED ACTIVITIES

Hugging Brothers

You'll need:

- Puppet templates

- Tagboard or heavy paper

- Paper, wallpaper, or fabric to fashion Yaakov's clothes

- Fur or cotton balls to fashion Eisav's clothes

- Flesh-tone construction paper

- Velcro

1. Using heavy paper or tagboard, fashion bodies for Yaakov and Eisav (approximately 8 inches tall), or trace the puppet templates.

2. Fashion clothing for Eisav and Yaakov using fur, fabric, or cotton balls.

3. For their legs, cut strips of construction paper, 2 × ½ inches. Attach to the bodies and bend at the ends to make feet.

4. For the arms, cut paper strips 3 × ½ inches. Attach the arms to the bodies.

5. Attach Velcro to the end of the arms. The brothers can wrap their arms around each other and hug!

Special Snack: Share the Love!

Celebrate the love between Eisav and Yaakov by cutting heart-shaped cookies from rolled cookie dough, baking them, and eating them! (See recipe in Appendix B.)

WALL TORAH

Invite children to fashion pictures of Yaakov, Eisav, wives, servants, children, soldiers, and sheep. Arrange them collage style with a desert background. Yaakov and Eisav should meet in the center of the picture.

LESSON 19

Joseph's Coat of Many Colors / Joseph's Dreams

כְּתֹנֶת פַּסִים

K'tonet Pasim

Genesis 37:1–11

INTRODUCTION

Yaakov has returned to Canaan with his wives, children, servants, and animals. His wife Racheil has died while giving birth to her second son, Binyamin. Yitzchak has also died, and Yaakov is now the leader of the Jewish people.

In this story, we deal with some very powerful emotions. Yaakov certainly loves all of his children very much, but he has a special feeling for Yoseif (יוֹסֵף), Racheil's first child. Yoseif reminds him of his beloved Racheil. Much to the dismay of the brothers, Yaakov shows favoritism to Yoseif. The brothers are jealous of their father's extra attention to this "special" child. Furthermore, Yoseif is boastful about having dreams that will predict events of the future. There are many highly charged emotions in the whole saga of Yoseif's life. This will set the stage for many interesting discussions. In relating to the children that Yaakov loved Yoseif more than the other brothers (or showed him favoritism), explain that this is not the way parents should generally behave. In future lessons, they will learn that God has special plans for Yoseif and that everything in Yoseif's life will happen for a special reason.

SYNOPSIS

After moving back to Canaan, Yaakov settles down with his family and establishes his home again. Yaakov is now the leader of the Jewish people. One day, Yaakov returns to his family with a beautiful *k'tonet pasim* (כְּתֹנֶת פַּסִּים), a coat of many beautiful colors, for Yoseif only. The brothers become very jealous of their brother Yoseif when Yaakov gives the coat to Yoseif. Making them even angrier, Yoseif tells his brothers of a dream in which he and his brothers were preparing sheaves of wheat in the field. Yoseif's sheaf stood up and all of the other eleven sheaves bowed down to his. The brothers asked him, "Do you mean that you'll rule over us someday?" Then, Yoseif told them of another dream. The sun, the moon, and the stars were bowing down to him. His brothers asked, "Do you mean that your father, your mother, and your brothers will bow down to you?" This was too much for the brothers to bear and they hated Yoseif.

CAST

- Yaakov

- Yoseif

- Yoseif's eleven brothers

SCENERY, COSTUMES, AND PROPS

- Canaan backdrop

- Tent and trees

- Beard for Yaakov

- Nice robe for Yaakov

- *K'tonet pasim* (coat of many colors)

- Robe for Yoseif

- Eleven sets of simple or tattered clothing and head coverings for brothers

- Eleven pinnies with pictures of wheat on them

- Picture of a sun

- Picture of a moon

- Eleven large stars or metallic material

- Optional: CD of *Joseph and the Amazing Technicolor Dreamcoat*. Use individual songs throughout the Yoseif unit. Play the CD as the children work or play.

SUGGESTED SCENE AND NARRATION

Yaakov is sitting by his tent, surrounded by his sons.

Yaakov: My sons, it is so nice to see you. I've just returned from the market.

Brothers: What did you bring home, father?

Yaakov: I bought this beautiful *k'tonet pasim* for Yoseif.

Brothers *(to each other):* Only for Yoseif? That makes us angry. We're jealous that he has such a beautiful coat and we are still wearing these plain clothes! *(Yoseif puts on the coat and struts around in front of his brothers. You may play "Joseph's Coat" from the CD as background music while Yoseif struts and the brothers sneer at Yoseif.)*

Yoseif: My brothers, I want to tell you about a dream I had. I believe my dreams tell about something that will happen in the future. *(Distribute wheat to Yoseif and the brothers. The brothers stand around Yoseif.)*

Yoseif: In my dream, we were all gathering wheat and tying it into sheaves. All of a sudden, my sheaf stood up and all of yours bowed down to mine. *(Brothers bow down.)*

Brothers: Are you telling us that someday we will bow down to you?

Narrator: Yoseif just smiles. *(Brothers make angry sounds.)* A few days later, Yoseif tells his brothers of another dream.

Yoseif: My brothers, I've had another dream. *(Distribute eleven stars, sun, and moon.)* In this dream, the sun, the moon ,and eleven stars stood around me. Then they all bowed down to me! *(Everyone bows down.)*

Brothers: Are you saying that your brothers will bow down to you AND your mother and father also?

Narrator: Yoseif just smiles.

Brothers *(to each other):* That's it! We can't stand this anymore! We need to get rid of him!

DISCUSSION QUESTIONS

- Can you imagine having eleven brothers and sisters? What do you think it would be like?

- Why did Yaakov have a special feeling for Yoseif? (*He was the son of Racheil.*)

- Why were Yoseif's brothers jealous? Do you think they were right to be jealous? Do you think Yaakov realized his brothers were jealous?

- Why did Yoseif's dreams make his brothers angry? (*Yoseif's dreams predicted that he would become more important than his brothers.*)

PUPPETS

Create a *k'tonet pasim* to add to the puppet bag. Use a 2 × 3–inch piece of striped fabric, wallpaper, or color stripes on a light color of construction paper.

RELATED ACTIVITIES

Personal *K'tonet Pasim*

You'll need:

- For each child, a pillowcase cut with room for a head and arms or a pinny cut from a solid piece of fabric or bed sheet.

- A variety of different-shaped sponges and rollers.

- Several different colors of paints set out in paper plates or pie plates.

Create stripes on the fabric using the rollers or sponges in patterns. Use many different colors. Have a "*Yom Yoseif*/Joseph Day" when all of the children can wear their coats for a Yoseif celebration.

Coat of Many Colors

You'll need:

- Coffee filters

- Liquid watercolors or food coloring mixed with water

1. Have the children dip coffee filters in a variety of liquid watercolors or food coloring.
2. After the filters dry, sketch a large picture of Yoseif.
3. Fill in Yoseif's coat by affixing the multitude of colorful coffee filters.

WALL TORAH

Sketch a large picture of Yoseif. Attach it to mural paper. Divide the picture into segments. Using markers, invite each child to design his or her own section.

LESSON 20

Joseph Is Thrown in the Pit / Joseph Goes to Egypt

יוֹסֵף בְּמִצְרַיִם

Yoseif B'Mitzrayim

Genesis 37:12–36

INTRODUCTION

In this lesson, we deal with very serious emotions. Yoseif's brothers are so angry with him that they want to kill him so they can be rid of him. At the last minute, they listen to one of the brothers, who decides that it would be terrible if they were to carry out their plans.

Once again, Yaakov is involved in a terrible "trick." In order to get rid of Yoseif, the brothers decide to play a heartbreaking trick on their father. They sell Yoseif into slavery. It is important to tell the children that, in the time of the Torah, people could be bought and sold as slaves. (When teaching about Pesach, this scene will explain how the Jews ended up in

Egypt. They will remain in Egypt for many years. During the time of Moses, they will all become slaves.)

Paroh (פַּרְעֹה), Pharoah, is the king of Egypt. At this time, there is no problem between *Paroh* and the Jews. This is also a different *paroh* than the one in the story of Mosheh (מֹשֶׁה), Moses. These events occur about 400 years before Mosheh.

SYNOPSIS

One day, Yoseif's brothers are out in the pasture taking care of the sheep. Yaakov sends Yoseif to see how they are. As they see him approaching, the brothers decide they should kill Yoseif, throw him in a *bor* (בּוֹר), pit, and say that a wild beast ate him. Then they won't have to listen to his dreams! Their oldest brother, Reuven, says, "We cannot kill him!" So, they take Yoseif's coat off and throw him in the pit while they decide his fate.

The brothers notice a caravan of *Yishmaeilim* (יִשְׁמָעֵאלִים), Ishmaelites, passing by. (The Ishmaelites were a group of people from a neighboring area.) They sell Yoseif to the Ishmaelites, who will be traveling on their camels to *Mitzrayim* (מִצְרַיִם), Egypt. In *Mitzrayim*, the Ishmaelites will sell Yoseif as a slave. The brothers then dip Yoseif's coat in the blood of a goat and bring the coat to their father. They tell Yaakov that Yoseif was killed by a wild animal. Yaakov is heartbroken and mourns for his son Yoseif.

CAST

- Yaakov

- Yoseif

- Yoseif's eleven brothers

- Ishmaelites

SCENERY, COSTUMES, AND PROPS

- Canaan backdrop

- A-frame ladder covered with a cloth or a large box to simulate a pit

- Robe for Yaakov

- *K'tonet pasim* for Yoseif

- Simple robes for the eleven brothers

- Sheep

- Desert robes for Ishmaelites that are different from those of the brothers

- Bag of coins

- Camel

SUGGESTED SCENE AND NARRATION

The scene takes place against the desert background in Canaan. The brothers, except for Yoseif, are gathered together, tending to the sheep. Off to the side, there is a pit. In another part of the room, Yaakov is talking to Yoseif.

Yaakov: Yoseif, your brothers are off in the meadows taking care of the sheep. Why don't you go to them and see how they're doing.

Yoseif: OK father. I'll go right now. *(Yoseif walks slowly toward the brothers.)*

A brother: Look, here comes the dreamer! I don't want to listen to any more of his dreams.

Another brother: Why don't we kill him! We'll throw him in a pit and tell everyone that a wild animal ate him.

Reuven: We can't kill our brother. No matter how much we dislike him, he's our brother. We can't do that!

A brother: OK, we won't kill him, but I sure would like to get rid of him.

Yoseif *(approaching his brothers):* Hi, guys. I came to see how you are doing.

A brother: Let's take off his beautiful coat and throw him in this pit! *(The brothers take Yoseif's coat and throw him in the pit.)*

A brother: Now we need to figure out how we can get rid of Yoseif without killing him.

Narrator: The brothers are gathered around the pit. Off in the distance is a group of Ishmaelite merchants with their camels.

A brother: Look, there's a caravan of Ishmaelites.

Y'hudah: Let's sell Yoseif to the merchants.

Ishmaelites: Greetings, friends. We're merchants traveling to *Mitzrayim*. We are buying things in Canaan to bring to *Mitzrayim* to sell. Do you have anything you would like to sell to us? We'll pay you with twenty pieces of silver. *(They hold up the bag of coins.)*

Brothers *(taking Yoseif out of the pit):* We would like to sell this fine, strong, young man. He would make a wonderful slave for somebody.

Ishmaelites: It's a deal. Here's your money. We'll travel to *Mitzrayim* and sell him there.

(Yoseif and the Ishmaelites walk away.)

A brother: Thank goodness we'll never have to see Yoseif again. We'll never have to listen to his crazy dreams again.

Another brother: What will we tell our father about Yoseif's disappearing?

A brother: We'll dip his coat in the blood of an animal and tell our father that Yoseif was eaten by a wild animal. *(A brother dips the coat in the blood of one of the sheep.)*

Narrator: The brothers bring the coat to Yaakov, who is sitting by his tent. *(Turn the "pit" upright to represent a tent.)*

A brother: Father, we're sorry to tell you that your beloved son Yoseif was eaten by a wild animal. All that's left is his torn coat.

Narrator: As Yaakov takes the coat, he brings it to his face.

Yaakov: Oh no! What will I do? I love him so much. I'll never see him again! *(Yaakov sobs.)*

DISCUSSION QUESTIONS

- Why didn't the brothers like Yoseif?

- Why did they decide not to kill him?

- How do you think Yoseif felt when he was thrown in the pit?

- What does it mean to be a slave?

- Why did the brothers decide to sell Yoseif to be a slave?

- Why do the brothers put blood on Yoseif's coat?

- How do you think Yoseif feels about being taken away from his family and his home?

PUPPETS

Create the following props, and add them to the puppet bag:

- An empty tissue box or large paper cup for a pit.

- A couple of pennies in a small plastic bag to use for the sale of Yoseif.

RELATED ACTIVITIES

Yoseif in the Pit

You'll need:

- 9 oz. paper or plastic cup

- Tagboard or construction paper

- Fabric or wallpaper for a *k'tonet pasim*

- Paper clips or Velcro

1. Fashion a picture of Yoseif, about 8 inches high, from the tagboard.

2. Fashion a *k'tonet pasim* for Yoseif from a piece of fabric or wallpaper, about 4 × 2 inches.

3. Use the cup as a pit. When Yoseif wears the *k'tonet pasim*, attached by clips or Velcro, he is walking outside the pit. When he is thrown in the pit, he takes off the *k'tonet pasim*.

WALL TORAH

Invite the children to create pictures of the eleven brothers, Yoseif, sheep, the sun, trees, and Ishmaelites with camels. Add a small cup for the pit on the mural, arranged collage style.

LESSON 21

Joseph Works for Potifar / Joseph in Jail

יוֹסֵף בְּבֵית הַסֹּהַר

Yoseif B'Veit HaSohar

Genesis 39:1–40:23

INTRODUCTION

In this lesson, we learn something about Yoseif's moral character. First, we learn that, even though Yoseif is a slave, he works very hard and is given a great deal of responsibility. Then he resists the temptation of a married woman, causing him to end up in the *Beit Sohar* (בֵּית סֹהַר), jail. While in jail, he tries to help his fellow men.

SYNOPSIS

Yoseif is brought to *Mitzrayim* and sold as a slave to a man named Potifar (פּוֹטִיפַר). Potifar is a very successful and important man. Potifar realizes that Yoseif is very capable and intelligent, so he puts Yoseif in charge of the entire household. He trusts Yoseif with all that he owns. Potifar's wife (her name isn't mentioned in the Torah) likes Yoseif a lot. She asks him if he would like to be her "boyfriend." Yoseif knows this is wrong and emphatically says "No!" each time she asks him. One day, when he is cleaning her room and no one is around, she chases him and pulls off his coat as he runs away. Potifar walks in as his wife is chasing Yoseif. Disappointed, she lies to her husband that Yoseif had actually chased her! Potifar is so furious that he has Yoseif thrown in the jail where the *Paroh* keeps his prisoners.

Some years after Yoseif goes to jail, *Paroh* becomes angry with two of the men who work for him. *Paroh*'s butler (who serves *Paroh* his wine) and baker are thrown into the same jail cell as Yoseif. Yoseif is given the responsibility of taking care of them. One night, both the butler and the baker have dreams. They tell Yoseif their dreams so he can interpret them. The butler tells his dream first. He says, "In my dream, there were three bunches of grapes in front of me. I squeezed them into *Paroh*'s cup and gave the cup of wine to him." Yoseif says, "The three bunches of grapes mean three days. In three days, *Paroh* will forgive you, and you will go back to your job serving wine to *Paroh*. Please, when you're free, tell *Paroh* that I am here, in jail, and can interpret dreams." Then the baker tells his dream. He says, "In my dream, I'm holding three baskets of bread above my head. There were birds eating the bread from the baskets." Yoseif says, "The three baskets mean three days. In three days, *Paroh* will have you killed." Three days later, *Paroh* sends his guards to the jail. Just as Yoseif had predicted, the butler is brought back to the palace to work for *Paroh* and the baker is killed. However, the butler forgets about Yoseif and does not tell *Paroh* about him. Yoseif stays in jail for another two years.

CAST

- Yoseif

- Potifar's wife

- Potifar

- Butler

- Baker

- Two guards

SCENERY, COSTUMES, AND PROPS

Note: Starting with this lesson, a distinction needs to be made between costumes for the prisoners and the Jewish slaves and for the Egyptians. Costumes for the slaves can be made from plain or tattered cloth. The Egyptians can wear more ornate and colorful robes.

- A new backdrop to look like *Mitzrayim*, Egypt—for example, a desert scene that looks somewhat different from Canaan, including buildings and cities built from large bricks (the pyramids were actually constructed long after the Jewish slaves left Egypt)

- A table to use as a bed

- Robe with a vest or coat over it for Yoseif

- A broom

- "Lovely" outfit (perhaps a pretty dress and lots of jewelry) for Potifar's wife

- "Rich"-looking robe for Potifar

- A-frame climbing equipment on its side to look like a jail cell

- Robes for the butler, baker, and two guards

- Baker's hat for the baker

- Three loaves of "stuffed bread" in a basket (see pages 153–154)

- Three bunches of grapes (plastic or fashioned from paper)

- A silver cup

SUGGESTED SCENE AND NARRATION

Against the backdrop of *Mitzrayim*.

Narrator:	Yoseif is a slave to Potifar. Yoseif is a very hard worker, so Potifar gives him lots of responsibility. One day, Yoseif is sweeping in the bedroom of Potifar's wife. She is resting in her bed.
Yoseif:	Good morning. Everybody is busy today and away from the house.
Wife:	Good morning, Yoseif. It's nice to see you. Yoseif, would you like to be my boyfriend?
Yoseif:	No! You're a married woman! That would be a terrible thing to do!
Wife:	Yoseif, please be my boyfriend!
Yoseif:	No!
Narrator:	Potifar's wife gets up and chases Yoseif around the bed. She grabs his coat and pulls it off. Potifar returns home and hears this commotion. Potifar enters looking very angry.
Potifar:	What's going on here?

Wife:	Oh, my husband, Yoseif wanted me to be his girlfriend, and I said, "No!" so he chased me around the room!
Potifar:	Yoseif, I trusted you. You've committed a terrible crime. Yoseif, you're going to jail! *(Replace the "bed" with a "jail." Turn the A-frame ladder on its side. The vertical bars will look like a jail. Yoseif sits in jail.)*
Narrator:	Yoseif stays in jail for quite a while. Even in jail, Yoseif works hard and tries to be helpful to the other prisoners. Eventually, two other men are put in the same jail cell with Yoseif. The two men are servants of the *Paroh.* One is the baker, and the other is the butler who serves wine to the *Paroh. (The baker and the butler sit next to Yoseif.)*
Yoseif:	Greetings, friends. I am Yoseif. Please let me know if I can help you while you're in jail.
Butler:	We're so tired. I think we'll go to sleep. *(Everyone goes to sleep.)*
Narrator:	In the morning, when they wake up, both the butler and the baker say they had very strange dreams.
Butler:	I had such a strange dream last night.
Baker:	So did I!
Yoseif:	Tell me what happened in your dreams, and I will tell you what your dreams mean.
Butler:	Great! In my dream, there were three bunches of grapes in front of me. I squeezed them into *Paroh*'s cup and gave the cup of wine to him.
Yoseif:	The three bunches of grapes mean three days. In three days, *Paroh* will forgive you, and you will go back to your job serving wine to *Paroh.*
Butler:	Thanks! That sounds great!
Baker:	Now, I'd like to tell you my dream, Yoseif. I hope you will give me a good message the way you gave the baker. In my

dream, I'm holding three baskets of bread above my head. There were birds eating the bread from the baskets.

Yoseif: The three baskets mean three days. In three days, *Paroh* will have you killed.

Narrator: Three days later, *Paroh* sends his guards to the jail. Just as Yoseif had predicted, the butler is brought back to the palace to work for *Paroh*. *(The guards come to the jail.)*

Guard 1: Butler, you need to come with me. *Paroh* wants you to serve him wine again.

Butler: Oh, Yoseif. Your prediction came true. Thank you!

Yoseif: Please, when you're free, tell *Paroh* that I am here, in jail, and can interpret dreams. Maybe I can help *Paroh* some day.

Guard 2: Baker, you need to come with me. You will not return to the palace. You will be killed today.

Yoseif: I'm sorry, Baker. That's what your dream meant.

Narrator: The guards take the butler and the baker away. However, the butler forgets about Yoseif and does not tell *Paroh* about him. Yoseif stays in jail for another two years.

DISCUSSION QUESTIONS

- Why do you think Yoseif worked so hard, even though he was a slave?

- Why do you think Yoseif did not argue with Potifar when his wife was lying?

- How do you think Yoseif feels about being able to interpret dreams?

- What clue in the butler's dream makes you think he will survive and go back to his job? *(The grapes added wine to the cup.)*

- What clue in the baker's dream makes you think he will not survive and not go back to his job? *(The birds took away the bread.)*

Torah Alive!

PUPPETS

Create the following props, and add them to the puppet bag:

- An appropriate piece of fabric for clothing for Potifar's wife.

- A small piece of fabric to be put on top of Yoseif's clothing. This can be "ripped" off as he is chased.

- An empty shoebox or tissue box to use for a bed and then stand upright for a jail.

- Bunches of grapes (plastic or paper).

- Loaves of "stuffed" bread (see below).

RELATED ACTIVITIES

What Can Happen When You Make Up Stories about Someone?

Pose these questions to the children: "What problems are caused when we are dishonest? What can happen when we tell untrue stories about people?" Generate ideas. List the ideas on chart paper. Stress the importance of being honest when we talk about other people.

Make "Stuffed" Bread

You'll need for each child:

- One pair of flesh-tone pantyhose or three knee-high stockings

- Batting

- Masking tape

1. If using pantyhose, cut the legs off, and cut each leg into two pieces.

2. Knot three of the pantyhose pieces or the three knee-high stockings at one end, leaving one end open.

3. Lightly stuff each piece with batting, and knot the ends.

4. Braid the pieces to look like challah.

5. Tuck the ends underneath, and secure with masking tape.

Make Miniature Loaves of Bread for Puppets

You'll need:

• Modeling clay

• Mod Podge

1. Give each child a small ball of modeling clay.

2. Ask the children to divide their ball of clay in thirds.

3. They may create any kind of creative loaf of bread out of each third.

4. Leave out to dry overnight.

5. For a shiny effect, paint with Mod Podge.

6. This project can also be done with a polymer clay and baked for a more durable product. Use the loaves with the puppets.

WALL TORAH

Have the children fashion and cut out pictures of Yoseif, the guards, the butler with three bunches of grapes, and the baker with three loaves of bread in a basket being eaten by birds. You may cut strips of black paper and place them vertically over the picture to resemble a jail cell.

LESSON 22

Pharaoh's Dreams
חֲלוֹמוֹת פַּרְעֹה
Chalomot Paroh

Genesis 41:1–43

INTRODUCTION

Yoseif stays in jail for another two years. His ability to interpret dreams not only saves his own life, but the lives of the inhabitants of an entire country and, ultimately, the Jewish people.

SYNOPSIS

One day, *Paroh* is troubled by two strange *chalomot* (חֲלוֹמוֹת), dreams. He sends for his magicians and wise men, but no one can interpret his dreams. Then, the butler remembers Yoseif and tells *Paroh* of his experience in jail. He tells *Paroh* how Yoseif had interpreted the dreams of the baker and himself and how the interpretations came true. *Paroh* sends for Yoseif to be brought from jail, and Yoseif appears before *Paroh*.

Paroh tells Yoseif of his dreams. He says, "In the first dream, I was standing by the bank of the Nile River. Out of the river, seven fat cows came to graze in the grass. Then, seven skinny and sickly cows came out of the river. The seven skinny cows ate up the seven fat cows, but they still looked skinny and sickly. In my other dream, I saw seven ears of fat and healthy corn growing on a single stalk. There were also seven skinny and shriveled ears of corn growing on one stalk. Then, the seven thin ears swallowed the seven fat ears of corn. No one can tell me what these dreams mean. Can you?"

Yoseif answers *Paroh*, "Your two dreams are actually one and the same. The seven fat cows and the seven healthy ears of corn mean that here in *Mitzrayim*, there will be seven years when there will be lots of food and good weather. The seven skinny cows and seven shriveled ears of corn mean that the seven good years will be followed by seven years of drought (no rain) and famine (no food). You need to find someone to supervise the collecting and storing of food during the seven good years. Then, during the seven bad years, this person will supervise the distribution of the food so the people of *Mitzrayim* won't starve."

Paroh says to Yoseif, "Since God has given you this ability to interpret the dreams, I want you to be in charge of overseeing this process. The only person who will be more powerful than you, in all of *Mitzrayim*, will be me. Here is my ring to show you how I trust you." *Paroh* also gives Yoseif a beautiful Egyptian robe and a gold necklace to wear as he takes charge of *Mitzrayim*.

CAST

- *Paroh*

- Yoseif

- Butler

- Guards

SCENERY, COSTUMES, AND PROPS

- *Mitzrayim* backdrop

- Royal robe for *Paroh*

- Throne for *Paroh*

- Simple clothes for Yoseif

- Tray and wine cup for butler

- Egyptian clothing for guards

- Pictures of cows (seven fat, seven skinny), held by children

- Pictures of corn (seven fat, seven skinny), held by children

- Blue fabric for a river

- "Gold" ring

- Special robe and necklace for Yoseif after he meets with *Paroh*

SUGGESTED SCENE AND NARRATION

The scene takes place against the backdrop of *Mitzrayim* in *Paroh*'s palace. *Paroh* is sitting on his throne. The butler is about to serve wine to *Paroh*.

Butler: *Paroh*, I have your wine for you.

Paroh: Oh, I can't drink wine today. I'm so tired.

Butler: Why are you so tired?

Paroh: I've been troubled by strange dreams, and I haven't been able to sleep well.

Butler: Have you found anyone to tell you what your dreams mean?

Paroh: I brought all of the magicians and wise men of *Mitzrayim* to the palace. None of them can tell me what these troubling dreams mean.

Butler: *Paroh*, when I was in the palace jail, there was a young Jewish man named Yoseif. The baker and I had dreams. He was able to tell us what they meant. Everything he told us came true.

Paroh: We must find this man. Guards!

Guards: Yes, *Paroh*.

Paroh: Go to the jail in the royal palace and find this man Yoseif. Bring him to me! *(The guards go away and come back with Yoseif.)*

Guards: Here is Yoseif.

Yoseif *(bows down to* Paroh*):* How may I help you, *Paroh*?

Paroh: I've had two troubling dreams.

Yoseif: Tell me about your dreams.

Paroh: In the first dream, I was standing by the bank of the Nile River. Out of the river, seven fat cows came to graze in the grass. Then, seven skinny and sickly cows came out of the river. The seven skinny cows ate up the seven fat cows, but they still looked skinny and sickly.

(Spread blue fabric in front of Paroh *and Yoseif to look like the river. Children with pictures of seven fat cows stand on one side. Children with pictures of seven skinny cows stand on the other side. The seven skinny cows cross over and make believe they are eating the seven fat cows.)*

In my other dream, I saw seven ears of fat and healthy corn growing on a single stalk. There were also seven skinny and shriveled ears of corn growing on one stalk. Then, the seven thin ears swallowed the seven fat ears of corn.

(Children with pictures of seven fat ears of corn stand on one side. Children with pictures of seven skinny ears of corn stand on the other side. The seven skinny ears of corn make believe they are eating the seven fat ears of corn.)

No one can tell me what these dreams mean. Can you?

Yoseif: Your two dreams are actually one and the same. The seven fat cows and the seven healthy ears of corn mean there will be, in *Mitzrayim*, seven years when there will be lots of food and good weather. The seven skinny cows and seven shriveled ears of corn mean that the seven good years will be followed by seven years when there will be a drought and there will not be any rain. This will cause a famine when there will not be enough food because the plants and animals will die.

Paroh: What should I do?

Yoseif: You need to find someone to be in charge of the collecting and storing of food during the seven good years. Then, during the seven bad years, this person will be in charge of giving out the food so the people of *Mitzrayim* won't starve.

Paroh: Yoseif, since God has given you this ability to interpret the dreams, I want you to be in charge of this process. The only person who will be more powerful than you, in all of *Mitzrayim*, will be me. Here is my ring to show you how I trust you. *(Paroh gives Yoseif a gold ring.)* Here is a beautiful robe and a gold necklace to wear as you take charge of *Mitzrayim*. *(Yoseif puts on the robe and necklace.)*

DISCUSSION QUESTIONS

- Dreams have been very important to Yoseif. Can you remember other times when dreams were important to him?

- Why do you think *Paroh*'s dreams were about cows and corn? *(These are things people need to feed their families.)*

- How will Yoseif's interpretations of *Paroh*'s dreams save the lives of many people?

PUPPETS

Create new and special robes for Yoseif and *Paroh* from pieces of fabric, paper, or wallpaper, and add them to the puppet bag.

RELATED ACTIVITIES

Paroh's Dreams

Gather cardboard tubes from the bottom of wire coat hangers or use slats from mini blinds. Each project will require four tubes or slats. Using one tube or slat for each of the following, attach pictures from magazines or original drawings of:

- Seven fat cows

- Seven skinny cows

- Seven fat ears of corn

- Seven skinny ears of corn

Use these props to retell *Paroh*'s dreams or use with puppet play.

Paroh's Ring

Paroh gave Yoseif his ring as a sign of the power that Yoseif would have in *Mitzrayim*. The children will enjoy twisting and molding silver or gold foil into a ring.

WALL TORAH

Invite the children to create and cut out pictures of Yoseif and *Paroh*, seven fat and seven skinny cows, and seven fat and seven skinny ears of corn. Place Yoseif and *Paroh* in the center of the mural paper. The students will have fun placing the skinny and fat cows on either side of a piece of blue tissue paper (river) and then placing the seven skinny and seven fat ears of corn opposite each other.

Yosef interprets Paroah's dream. He predicts 7 years plenty of food followed by 7 years of drought.

LESSON 23

Joseph and His Brothers Reunited

יוֹסֵף וְאֶחָיו

Yoseif V'Echav

Genesis 41:44–42:38

INTRODUCTION

Just as Yoseif has predicted, there are seven years of plenty in *Mitzrayim*. During those years, Yoseif supervises the gathering and storing of the food in warehouses in the cities. A very large amount of food is collected. During this time, Yoseif marries and has two sons, Efrayim (אֶפְרַיִם) and M'nasheh (מְנַשֶּׁה). When the drought and famine occur, it affects all of the lands in the area. However, it becomes known that the people of *Mitzrayim* are not starving because they are receiving food from Yoseif. Many years have passed since Yoseif last saw his brothers. He is now a grown man, and he dresses as an important royal Egyptian leader. He no longer looks like the boy who was sold into slavery by his brothers.

The next lesson is a continuation of the story presented in this lesson, using the same costumes and props. They can easily be combined, creating a longer lesson, if you prefer.

SYNOPSIS

In Canaan, which is near *Mitzrayim*, Yaakov and his family are affected by the famine. Yaakov tells his sons to go to *Mitzrayim* to get food to prevent the family from starving. All of the sons, except Binyamin (בִּנְיָמִן), the youngest, go to *Mitzrayim*. Yaakov does not want to send Binyamin because he is the only remaining son of Racheil.

When the brothers arrive in *Mitzrayim*, they go to Yoseif, since he is the person who distributes the food. As they approach Yoseif, they don't recognize him, and they bow low to the ground. When Yoseif sees them, he recognizes them but acts like a stranger. "Where do you come from?" he asks. "From the land of Canaan," they answer. Yoseif accuses them of being spies. They reply that they are all brothers, born to the same father. They tell Yoseif, "We used to be twelve brothers. The youngest is back with our father, and one [Yoseif] is already dead." Yoseif says to them, "So, you **are** spies! Unless your youngest brother comes here, you will not be allowed to leave from here!" Yoseif then changes his mind and says that if one brother stays behind, the others may bring food back to their starving families, and when the youngest brother comes to *Mitzrayim*, Yoseif will allow them all to be free. The brothers start to argue among themselves, blaming this terrible fate on having "killed" their brother. They don't realize that Yoseif actually understands their language and turns away because he is crying. Unknown to the brothers, Yoseif gives his guards instructions to fill their bags with grain, and to return the money in each brother's sack. Shimon (שִׁמְעוֹן) stays in *Mitzrayim*.

When the nine brothers return to Yaakov in Canaan, they realize that they all have their money in their sacks. They are afraid that Yoseif will think they've been dishonest and that they really are spies. Yaakov will not allow the brothers to take Binyamin to *Mitzrayim* because he has already lost Yoseif and is not willing to lose Binyamin as well.

CAST

- Yoseif

- Yoseif's eleven brothers

- Yaakov

- Guards

SCENERY, COSTUMES, AND PROPS

Two parts of the room are needed for the next two lessons because the family travels back and forth between Canaan and *Mitzrayim*.

In one part of the room:

- Backdrop of *Mitzrayim*

- Royal robe for Yoseif

- Egyptian clothes for guards

In a second part of the room:

- Backdrop of Canaan

- Tent

- Tattered clothes for Yaakov and the eleven brothers

- Ten empty sacks (grocery bags) for the brothers going to Egypt

SUGGESTED SCENE AND NARRATION

In Canaan, Yaakov is sitting by his tent, surrounded by his eleven remaining sons.

Yaakov: My sons, there's hardly any food left. We will be starving soon. I hear there is plenty of food in *Mitzrayim*.

Brother: You're right, father. We will all travel to *Mitzrayim* and bring back sacks of food.

Yaakov: Binyamin will stay with me. I've already lost my son Yoseif. I cannot bear to lose Binyamin. Now put the money in your sacks, and return with food. *(The ten sons take their sacks and walk slowly to* Mitzrayim.)

In *Mitzrayim*...

Narrator: When the brothers arrive in *Mitzrayim*, they go to Yoseif, since he is the person who distributes the food. As they approach Yoseif, they don't recognize him, and they bow low to the ground. When Yoseif sees them, he recognizes them but acts like a stranger.

Yoseif: Where do you come from?

Brothers: We are from the land of Canaan.

Yoseif: Oh really! I think you're spies!

Brothers: Oh no! We are all brothers, born to the same father. We used to be twelve brothers. The youngest is back with our father, and one is already dead.

Yoseif: So, you **are** spies! Unless your youngest brother comes here, you will not be allowed to leave from here! You'll stay here until I tell you that you may leave.

Narrator: A few days pass, and Yoseif changes his plans.

Yoseif: If one brother stays behind, the rest of you may bring food back to your starving families. When your youngest brother comes to *Mitzrayim*, I will allow all of you to be free.

Narrator:	The guards tie up one brother, Shimon. The brothers start to argue among themselves, blaming this terrible situation on having "killed" their brother. They don't realize that Yoseif actually understands their language and turns away because he is crying.
Brothers:	You see, this is all happening because we killed Yoseif! It was a very bad idea! *(Yoseif turns away as he hears this.)*
Yoseif:	Guards, come here so I can give you instructions. *(To the guards only.)* Fill their bags with grain, and put their money back in each sack.
Brothers:	Thank you. When we return, we will bring our brother. *(The nine brothers walk slowly back to Canaan.)*

Back in Canaan.

Yaakov:	It's good to see you, my sons. Where is your brother Shimon?
Brothers:	He is still in *Mitzrayim*. If we want more food and our brother Shimon, we must bring Binyamin to *Mitzrayim*.
Yaakov:	I will not allow you to take Binyamin. He must stay here. I can't bear to lose him.
Narrator:	The brothers open their sacks to show the food to their father.
Brothers:	Oh no! The money for the food is still in the sacks! Now they will really think we are spies!

DISCUSSION QUESTIONS

• Why did the brothers need to travel to *Mitzrayim*? How do you think they traveled there?

• Why did Binyamin stay behind? *(Yaakov can't bear to lose another son, especially Racheil's son.)*

- Why do you think Yoseif plays a trick on his brothers?

- Why do you think Yoseif wants to see Binyamin?

- Why are the brothers upset that the money is still in their bags?

PUPPETS

Use small plastic or paper bags for sacks, and add them to the puppet bag.

RELATED ACTIVITIES

Food Collection

What do we do in our own communities to make sure there is enough food for everyone? What happens when families run out of food?

Tell the children about local food pantries and how they help families in need of food. Have the children generate a list of the food required to feed a needy family for one day. Each child will be assigned to donate a specific nonperishable food item. Decorate a large cardboard box to hold all the food. A valuable problem-solving discussion is how the box will be delivered. Some food pantries will pick up donations. Perhaps the children can arrange to deliver the box as a class and visit the facility. Brainstorm with the children whether there is anything else they could do to help the food pantry. They often suggest that the *tzedakah* (צְדָקָה) they collect for a certain period of time could be donated.

WALL TORAH

Invite the children to fashion and cut out pictures of Yoseif and the ten brothers. Yoseif should be in "royal" clothing and the brothers in very plain clothes, perhaps in a bowing position. Arrange the brothers around Yoseif, collage style, on mural paper.

LESSON 24

Jacob's Family is Reunited

יַעֲקֹב וּבָנָיו הִתְאַחֲדוּ

Yaakov U'Vanav Hitachadu

Genesis 43:1–47:27

INTRODUCTION

The famine in the land is very severe. When Yaakov's family finishes the food brought back by the brothers, Yaakov wants them to return to *Mitzrayim* for more. Y'hudah (יְהוּדָה) reminds his father that they cannot return to *Mitzrayim* without their brother Binyamin, and he takes responsibility for Binyamin's safety. As they prepare to leave, they take double the money in case the first money was left there by mistake, as well as gifts. Yoseif now plays a terrible trick on the brothers before revealing his true identity. In the end, we see how Yoseif forgives his brothers, believing that God has planned for all of these events to happen so Yoseif could save the Jewish people.

SYNOPSIS

The brothers, including Binyamin, return to *Mitzrayim*. They are afraid they will be in trouble for having the money from the first visit in their sacks. However, they are treated very nicely, and they are invited to Yoseif's home for dinner. Shimon is returned to the family. Upon seeing Yoseif, they once again bow to him, and give him the gifts they have brought. As soon as Yoseif sees them, he asks, "How is your father?" When Yoseif sees Binyamin, he is overcome with emotion and needs to leave the room to cry in private. When he returns to the dinner, he instructs his servant to fill his brothers' bags with food, put the money back in the bags, and put his silver cup in Binyamin's bag.

The next day, the brothers begin their journey back to Canaan. Just as they leave the city, Yoseif sends his servant after them. The servant stops them and tells them that Yoseif's silver cup has been stolen. He says to the brothers, "Why did you repay good with evil?" The brothers deny any wrongdoing and offer their bags for inspection. The servant searches their bags, beginning with the oldest brother and ending with the youngest. As planned, the goblet is found in Binyamin's bag.

When the brothers return to Yoseif's home, they plead for his compassion. Yoseif tells them, "Only Binyamin will have to stay behind as my slave. The rest of you may return to your father." Y'hudah pleads with Yoseif to let Binyamin return to their father and offers to stay in his place. Yoseif can't control his emotions anymore and asks for all of his servants to leave the room. Yoseif cries very hard and finally says to his brothers, "I am Yoseif whom you sold to Egypt. Don't blame yourselves for what has happened. God sent me here to save your lives from the famine." Yoseif is very anxious to see his father, Yaakov, and tells his brothers, "Now, go to Canaan and bring back your families and your animals. Bring my father back quickly." Yoseif sends wagons to make their trip easier. Yoseif hugs his brother Binyamin, and they cry together. He kisses all of his brothers as they cry with him and talk to him.

Yaakov and Yoseif are reunited, and they cry as they hug each other. Yaakov is very old and is grateful for seeing Yoseif again before he dies. Yaakov comes to Egypt with seventy family members. The family is given a special area of *Mitzrayim* called Goshen where they can live and raise their families and their sheep.

CAST

- Yoseif

- Yoseif's eleven brothers

- Yaakov

- Two servants

SCENERY, COSTUMES, AND PROPS

In one part of the room:

- Backdrop of *Mitzrayim*

- Royal robe for Yoseif

- Tattered clothing for Shimon

- Egyptian clothing for the two servants

- Silver cup

In a second part of the room:

- Backdrop of Canaan

- Tent

- Tattered clothing for Yaakov and the ten brothers

- Ten empty sacks for the brothers

SUGGESTED SCENE AND NARRATION

In Canaan, Yaakov is sitting at his tent, surrounded by his ten sons.

Yaakov: The famine in the land is very bad. There's very little food left. You need to return to *Mitzrayim* to buy more food.

Y'hudah: Remember, Father, we cannot return to *Mitzrayim* without our brother Binyamin.

Yaakov: You can't take Binyamin!

Y'hudah: I will make sure Binyamin is safe.

Yaakov: Take double the amount of money with you in case the first money was left in the sacks by mistake. Also, take some gifts with you for the great leader. *(The ten brothers take their sacks and slowly walk to* Mitzrayim.)

(In Mitzrayim, *the brothers go to Yoseif. They bow in front of him.)*

Yoseif *(hiding his excitement):* I see your brother Binyamin is with you. How is your father?

Brothers: He is well.

Narrator: Yoseif becomes very emotional and needs to leaves the room to cry in private. *(Yoseif leaves and we can hear him crying.)* When Yoseif is able to stop crying, he returns to the room.

Yoseif *(to his servant):* Take these men to my house and we will have dinner. *(To the brothers)* Shimon will join you now that you brought your brother Binyamin.

Narrator: The brothers sit down to have dinner. Yoseif whispers to his servant.

Yoseif: Fill their sacks with food. Put their money on top. Put my silver cup in the sack of the youngest one. *(The servant puts the silver cup in Binyamin's sack.)*

Narrator:	The next day, the brothers begin their journey back to Canaan. Just as they leave the city, Yoseif sends his servant after them.
Yoseif:	Go after those men and stop them! Someone stole my silver cup! *(The servant chases after the brothers and stops them.)*
Servant:	My master's silver cup has been stolen! Why did you repay good with evil? He was so nice to you, and you steal from him. That's very mean!
Brothers:	We're innocent! Please check our bags if you don't believe us!
Servant:	Fine! Open your bags so we can search for the cup. We'll start with the oldest brother and finish with the youngest.
Narrator:	The servant searches the bags.
Servant *(taking the silver cup out of Binyamin's sack):*	I found the cup! It's in the sack of Binyamin! You're all coming back with me! *(The brothers go back to Yoseif's home.)*
Brothers:	We didn't steal your silver cup! It's a mistake! Please understand!
Yoseif:	Only Binyamin will have to stay behind as my slave. The rest of you may return to your father.
Narrator:	The brothers bow down to the ground and plead for him to let Binyamin go free.
Y'hudah:	Please let Binyamin return to our father. Our father didn't want us to bring Binyamin, but he knew we would starve if we didn't come back for food. We told him you wouldn't give us food unless we brought Binyamin. I promised I would protect Binyamin. Please, take me as a slave instead!
Narrator:	Yoseif can't control his emotions anymore and asks for all of his servants to leave the room. Yoseif cries very hard.
Yoseif *(to his brothers):*	I am Yoseif, whom you sold to Egypt.
Narrator:	The brothers are so shocked that they cannot speak.

Yoseif: Don't blame yourselves for what has happened to me. God sent me here to save your lives from the famine. Now, go to Canaan and bring back your families and your animals. You will live in the area of Goshen, where you can take care of your flocks. I will send wagons so you can bring my father back quickly.

Narrator: Yoseif hugs his brother Binyamin, and they cry together. He kisses all of his brothers as they cry with him and talk to him. *(The brothers hug Yoseif.)* The brothers return to Canaan and gather their families and animals. They journey to *Mitzrayim.* Yaakov and Yoseif are reunited, and they cry as they hug each other. *(Yoseif and Yaakov hug.)*

Yaakov: I am very old, and I'm so grateful for seeing you again before I die.

Narrator: Yaakov comes to Egypt with seventy family members. They live there in peace for many years.

DISCUSSION QUESTIONS

- Why do you think Yoseif cries when he sees his brothers come back with Binyamin?

- Why do you think Yoseif gives instructions to put the cup in Binyamin's sack? Why do think Yoseif played such a mean trick on his brothers?

- Why did Y'hudah volunteer to remain behind as a prisoner?

- Why isn't Yoseif angry with his brothers?

- What do you think the brothers told Yaakov?

- Think about all the things that happened to Yoseif. How were they evidence of God's plan?

PUPPETS

Because there are so many male characters in this story, you can use the female puppets for some of the brothers. Use the "sacks" made out of small plastic or paper bags.

RELATED ACTIVITIES

Yoseif's Silver Cup

Cover a paper or plastic cup with silver aluminum foil. The children may hide the cup in a grocery bag filled with "grain."

WALL TORAH

Invite the children to fashion pictures of Yoseif in royal clothing and his brothers in tattered clothing, carrying sacks. Create an Egyptian/palatial background. Cut out pictures, and affix collage style.

LESSON 25

Jacob Blesses Ephraim and Manasseh

יַעֲקֹב מְבָרֵךְ אֶת אֶפְרַיִם וּמְנַשֶּׁה

Yaakov M'vareich et Efrayim U'M'nasheh

Genesis 47:28–48:22

INTRODUCTION

Yaakov has lived in *Mitzrayim* for seventeen years. He is now very old and wants to say his final words to his family. He blesses Yoseif's sons and asks Yoseif to promise that he (Yaakov) will be buried in Canaan with his ancestors. Yaakov blesses the boys by telling them that future generations will say, "May God make you like Efrayim and M'nasheh," which has become the very blessing parents use to bless their own sons before Shabbat, holidays, and special occasions. For daughters, the blessing is "May God make you like our mothers, Sarah, Rivkah, Racheil, and Lei-ah."

SYNOPSIS

When Yoseif is told that his father is very ill, he brings his two sons, Efrayim and M'nasheh, to Yaakov. Yaakov is very weak and sits up in bed. Yaakov tells Yoseif, "God appeared to me in Canaan and blessed me. God said the Jewish people would become a large community and the land of Canaan would be for the Jewish people forever." When Yaakov realizes that Yoseif's sons are with him, he asks that they come close to him so he can bless them. Yaakov hugs them and says, "Yoseif, I never expected to see you again. And now, God has even let me see your children as well." Yoseif brings his sons in front of Yaakov. Yaakov places his hands on the heads of Efrayim and M'nasheh. He begins his blessing by saying, "The God who has been the God of my fathers, Avraham and Yitzchak, the God who has been my God, bless these boys. May my name be remembered through these children, and may they be the fathers of many children." He then says that all Jews, *Yisrael*, will bless their sons with this blessing he will give them: *"Y'simcha Elohim k'Efrayim v'chi'M'nasheh,"* "May God make you like Efrayim and M'nasheh." Yaakov is able to face the end of his life knowing he has passed on a tradition from his fathers through himself and on to his grandchildren.

CAST

- Yaakov

- Yoseif

- Efrayim

- M'nasheh

SCENERY, COSTUMES, AND PROPS

- Background of *Mitzrayim*

- Bed (e.g., table or floor) and pillow for Yaakov

- Egyptian clothing for Yaakov, Yoseif, Efrayim, and M'nasheh

SUGGESTED SCENE AND NARRATION

Narrator: Yoseif is told that his father, Yaakov, is very ill, and he brings his two sons, Efrayim and M'nasheh to see him. They stand by his bedside. Yaakov is very weak and sits up in bed.

Yaakov: Yoseif, God appeared to me in Canaan, when I wrestled through the night with an angel, and then God blessed me. God said the Jewish people would become a large community and the land of Canaan would be a Jewish home forever.

Yoseif: Yes, father.

Yaakov: Who is with you, Yoseif?

Yoseif: Father, these are my sons, Efrayim and M'nasheh.

Yaakov: Please come close to me so I can bless you.

Narrator: Yaakov hugs Efrayim and M'nasheh.

Yaakov: Yoseif, I never expected to see you again. And now, God has even let me see your children as well.

Narrator: Yoseif brings his sons in front of Yaakov. Yaakov places his hands on the heads of Efrayim and M'nasheh.

Yaakov: The God who has been the God of my fathers, Avraham and Yitzchak, the God who has been my God, bless these boys. May my name be remembered through these children, and may they be the fathers of many children. All Jews, *Yisrael*, will bless their sons with this blessing I will give you: *Y'simcha Elohim k'Efrayim v'chi'M'nasheh,* May God make you like Efrayim and M'nasheh.

Narrator: Yaakov is able to face the end of his life knowing he has passed on a tradition from his fathers through himself and on to his grandchildren.

DISCUSSION QUESTIONS

- Why is Yaakov happy to see his grandchildren?

- Why is it a nice thing for parents to bless their children and grandchildren?

- If you were going to make a blessing for your parents, grandparents, or siblings, what types of things would you wish for them?

PUPPETS

All personalities in this lesson are males. The children may dress the puppets in robes as Yaakov, Yoseif, Efrayim, and M'nasheh.

RELATED ACTIVITIES

Blessing the Children

It is said that when you are a teacher, your students are like your children. A beautiful custom to initiate after learning about Efrayim and M'nasheh would be to bless the children each Friday.

Parents' Blessing of the Children

You'll need:

- 9 × 12– and 12 × 18–inch construction paper

- A copy of the blessing for each child (page 186)

- Glue

- Markers

1. On the top of the 9 x 12–inch paper, trace the child's two hands facing each other. Have the child color the hands.

2. The student will draw a self-portrait below the hands. (You may also use a photo.)

3. Center and affix the 9 × 12–inch paper onto a contrasting piece of 12 × 18–inch paper.

4. Adjust the layout and size of the blessing, and affix it to the bottom portion of the "frame."

5. Send this blessing home to be used on Friday nights and holidays. Encourage parents to place this artwork on the table with other Shabbat and holiday ritual objects. The parents may start a new custom or continue a very old one!

Birkat Y'ladim/Blessing the Children

FOR A BOY

יְשִׂמְךָ אֱלֹהִים
כְּאֶפְרַיִם וְכִמְנַשֶּׁה.

Y'simcha Elohim k'Efrayim v'chi'M'nasheh.

May God inspire you to live in the tradition of Ephraim and Manasseh, who carried forward the life of our people.

FOR A GIRL

יְשִׂמֵךְ אֱלֹהִים כְּשָׂרָה,
רִבְקָה, לֵאה, וְרָחֵל.

Y'simeich Elohim k'Sarah, Rivkah, Lei-ah, v'Racheil.

May God inspire you to live in the tradition of Sarah, Rebekah, Leah, and Rachel, who carried forward the life of our people.

FOR BOTH

יְבָרֶכְךָ יְיָ וְיִשְׁמְרֶךָ.
יָאֵר יְיָ פָּנָיו אֵלֶיךָ
וִיחֻנֶּךָ.
יִשָּׂא יְיָ פָּנָיו אֵלֶיךָ
וְיָשֵׂם לְךָ שָׁלוֹם.

Y'varehch'cha Adonai v'yishm'rehcha.
Yaeir Adonai panav eilehcha
vichunehcha.
Yisa Adonai panav eilehcha
v'yaseim l'cha shalom.

May God bless you and keep you. May God look kindly upon you, and be gracious to you. May God reach out to you in tenderness, and give you peace.

WALL TORAH

Invite the children to fashion pictures of Yoseif, Efrayim, and M'nasheh, and Yaakov in bed reaching for his grandchildren. An interesting addition to the mural would be to put two handprints facing each other on the top of the mural to signify the blessing.

LESSON 26

Baby Moses
מֹשֶׁה הַתִּינוֹק
Mosheh HaTinok

Exodus 1:1–2:10

INTRODUCTION

Four hundred years have passed since the time of Yoseif. At first, the Jews lived very peacefully in *Mitzrayim*. Each time a *paroh* died, his son would become the next *paroh*. For a long time, the *parohs* were very grateful to Yoseif for having saved the people of *Mitzrayim* from starvation. Eventually, there is a new *paroh* who doesn't know about Yoseif. This new *paroh* is afraid the Jewish population will grow too large. He is afraid that someday they might band together and fight against him. At first, he decides to make them slaves. The Jewish slaves are referred to as *B'nei Yisrael*, the Children of Israel (Yaakov's new name). *Paroh* forces the Jews to build the cities of Pithom and Raamses. Despite the rigorous work, the Jews continue to have many babies. *Paroh* orders that the midwives should kill all the Jewish male babies, but they do not. Then *Paroh* gives his soldiers orders that Jewish baby boys are to be drowned in the river Nile. The girls are allowed to live because *Paroh* can't imagine that the Jewish girls would grow up to fight against him. His soldiers keep track of the Jewish women who are expecting babies to make sure only the girls survive.

In this lesson, the children will learn how Moses escaped this decree and was saved by *Paroh*'s daughter. In the Torah, *Paroh*'s daughter does not have a name. In the Midrash, the great Sages gave her the name Batya (בַּתְיָה), which means "daughter of God." These great teachers felt that God must have had a role in placing her at the river's edge at the moment when she could save this child who would grow up to save the Jewish people. Additionally, it would be interesting to point out that, in the time of the Torah, all women had to nurse their babies. (Young children have generally seen a mother nursing her child.) Generally, only a woman who has recently given birth can nurse a baby. *Paroh*'s daughter had not given birth, so she was not able to nurse the baby.

This story begins the second book of the Torah, called Exodus or *Sh'mot* (שְׁמוֹת). This book describes the plight of the Jewish slaves in *Mitzrayim*, their flight from *Mitzrayim*, the wandering in the wilderness, and the receiving of the laws on Mount Sinai.

SYNOPSIS

Paroh's soldiers are ordered to kill all Jewish male newborn babies by drowning them in the Nile River. One Jewish woman, Yocheved, gives birth and hides her son from the soldiers. After three months, when she can no longer hide him, she makes a basket, covers it with pitch, and places him among the reeds near the riverbank. The baby's sister, Miryam, hides in the reeds to watch what will happen.

Paroh's daughter and her maids come to the river to bathe. *Paroh*'s daughter sees the basket and asks her maid to get it. When she opens the basket and sees the baby boy crying, she knows it must be a Hebrew child. Miryam approaches *Paroh*'s daughter and asks if she would like a

Hebrew woman to nurse the baby. *Paroh*'s daughter agrees, and Miryam brings her mother. Yocheved takes the baby home, nurses him, and raises him. When he grows up, Yocheved brings him to *Paroh*'s daughter to live with her in *Paroh*'s palace. *Paroh*'s daughter names him Mosheh (מֹשֶׁה, Moses) which means "I drew (took) him out of the water."

CAST

- Yocheved

- Miryam

- *Paroh*'s daughter

- Two maids for *Paroh*'s *daughter*

SCENERY, COSTUMES, AND PROPS

- *Mitzrayim* backdrop

- Blue cloth on floor to represent the Nile River

- Egyptian princess clothing and jewels for *Paroh*'s daughter

- Egyptian clothing (harem pants and top) for two maids

- Tree, bush, or tall plant

- Simple robes for Miryam and Yocheved

- Doll in a basket for baby Mosheh

SUGGESTED SCENE AND NARRATION

The scene occurs against the backdrop of *Mitzrayim*. Place a blue cloth on the floor to represent the Nile River. *Paroh*'s daughter is preparing to bathe in the river, accompanied by her maids. There is a bush or tree off to the side. Miryam is hiding behind it with her mother, Yocheved, nearby. Yocheved is holding a basket with a baby in it.

Narrator: *Paroh* was afraid of the Jewish people. He made them slaves and ordered that all Jewish baby boys be killed. Yocheved, a Jewish woman, gave birth to a baby boy. She hid him from *Paroh*'s soldiers. When he was three months old, she couldn't hide him any longer. She took a basket and covered the outside with tar so it would float. She wrapped her son in a blanket, put him in the basket, and went to the river's edge with her daughter, Miryam. *(You may play "Yocheved's Lament" from* Mostly Matzah *by Fran Avni.)*

Yocheved: Miryam, I'm going to place the basket here among the bulrushes. I'm so sad to see him go. *(Yocheved kisses the baby.)*

Miryam: I'll stand nearby and watch to see what happens to him.

Narrator: *Paroh*'s daughter goes into the river to take her bath while her maids stand on the bank of the river.

Paroh*'s daughter (speaking to her maids):* Look! There is a basket in the bulrushes. Please get the basket and bring it to me.

Maid: Here is the basket.

Paroh*'s daughter (opening the basket):* There is a baby boy in here. He's so sweet. This must be a Hebrew child.

Miryam (coming out from behind the bushes): You will need to feed this baby. Would you like me to find a Hebrew woman to nurse the baby for you?

Paroh*'s daughter:* Yes, thank you. *(Miryam runs to get her mother.)*

Miryam: Mother, the princess needs a woman to nurse the baby. Come with me. You will be able to nurse your own child. *(Miryam brings Yocheved to Paroh's daughter.)*

Paroh's daughter: Please take this baby and nurse him for me. When he grows up, you will bring him back to me.

Yocheved: I will be happy to nurse him and raise him.

Narrator: Yocheved raises the baby. When he grows up, she gives him back to *Paroh*'s daughter. *Paroh*'s daughter gives him an Egyptian name, Mosheh, which means "I took him out of the water." He continues to live in *Paroh*'s palace as part of the royal family.

DISCUSSION QUESTIONS

- Why do you think *Paroh* was afraid of the Jewish people? (*Perhaps he was afraid because they didn't worship idols like the Egyptians. They were different from the Egyptians.*)

- Why did *Paroh* make the Jewish people slaves?

- How do you think *Paroh*'s daughter knew that the baby she found was Jewish? Why do you think she wanted to save him?

PUPPETS

Hopefully, there's still room in your puppet bag! Add the following props:

- New clothing for *Paroh*'s daughter. Use wallpaper or fabric scraps. Decorate with sequins or glitter.

- A basket, including baby Mosheh, made from craft foam or construction paper.

- A piece of blue paper for the river.

RELATED ACTIVITIES

Baby Mosheh in the Basket

You'll need:

- Small green woven basket from a package of strawberries or tomatoes

- Narrow strips of brown construction paper to make "reeds"

- Craft foam, paper, or pipe cleaners

1. Have the children weave the "reeds" in and out of the slits in the baskets.

2. Have the children fashion baby Mosheh from craft foam, construction paper, or pipe cleaners, then place the baby in the basket.

3. If you have a water table in your room, set the basket in a plastic dish and float the basket down the "river." Attach some "reeds" to the sides of the table. Some of the children may dress as Yocheved, Miryam, and *Paroh*'s daughter and stand by the table.

Special Snack: What's in the Basket?

The children will enjoy filling "baskets" for a special treat. Using the cookie dough recipe in Appendix B, make thumbprint cookies. Make a depression in the dough with your thumb before cooking. Fill the "baskets" made by your thumbprints with jelly or a candy kiss. Yum!

WALL TORAH

Invite the children to cover the bottom half of a piece of mural paper with blue tissue paper to represent the Nile River. Children may fashion and cut out:

- Bulrushes by cutting strips of green paper and adding brown tips

- Miryam and Yocheved hiding behind the bush

- *Paroh*'s daughter in the river

- The maids on the river bank

- A sun

Yocheved put her baby in a basket and into the Nile River. Paroh's daughter finds him. Miriam gets her mother, Yocheved, to nurse the baby.

LESSON 27

The Burning Bush
הַסְּנֶה הַבֹּעֵר
HaSneh HaBo-eir

Exodus 2:11–4:18

INTRODUCTION

Mosheh has been nursed by his birth mother, Yocheved, and is now a prince in *Paroh*'s palace with his adoptive mother, the daughter of *Paroh*. He has not lived the life of the slaves, but he seems to have empathy for their situation.

While Mosheh is in Midian, *B'nei Yisrael* are miserable and cry out to God. God hears the cries of the Israelites and remembers the covenant (promise) with Avraham, Yitzchak, and Yaakov.

SYNOPSIS

When Mosheh grows up, he goes out among the slaves to see their hard work. He sees an Egyptian beating a Hebrew slave. He hits the Egyptian to make him stop, but he hits him so hard that the Egyptian is killed. He knows *Paroh* will kill him for this crime, so he runs away to the land of Midian. Mosheh stays in Midian and marries Tziporah (צִפֹּרָה), Yitro's daughter.

One day, Mosheh is tending Yitro's flock of sheep. The sheep wander into the wilderness, and Mosheh follows. Mosheh sees a bush that is on fire (הַסְּנֶה הַבֹּעֵר), but isn't being destroyed. Mosheh says, "I must turn to look at this marvelous sight. Why doesn't the bush burn up?" God calls to him out of the bush, "Mosheh, Mosheh." Mosheh answers, "Here I am." God tells him not to come closer and to take off his sandals because the place on which he is standing is holy ground. God says, "I am the God of your father, the God of Avraham, the God of Yitzchak, and the God of Yaakov." Mosheh hides his face because he is afraid to look at God. God tells Mosheh, "I have seen the struggle of My people in *Mitzrayim*. I hear their cries because of the Egyptian taskmasters. I know about their suffering. I have come down to rescue them from the Egyptians and bring them to a beautiful land, a land flowing with milk and honey, the land of Canaan." God tells Mosheh that he will be sent to *Paroh* and will ask him to free the Israelites from Egypt. When Mosheh expresses concern as to why he was chosen for this task, God assures him, "I will be with you." Mosheh is also concerned that *B'nei Yisrael*, the Israelites, won't believe that God spoke to him and won't follow him. God tells Mosheh to throw down his rod (stick). Mosheh drops the rod on the ground, and the stick turns into a snake. Mosheh backs away from the snake, but God tells him to grab it by the tail. As he does, the snake turns back into a rod. God tells Mosheh that this is a sign that God is with him, and when *B'nei Yisrael* see this, they will follow him. Mosheh is also concerned that he is not a very good speaker. How would he speak to *Paroh*? God assures him, "I will be with you and give you the words." God also tells Mosheh that he can bring his brother, Aharon (אַהֲרֹן), who speaks well. God will tell Mosheh, Mosheh will tell Aharon, and Aharon will speak to *Paroh* and *B'nei Yisrael*.

CAST

- Mosheh

- Egyptian taskmaster

- Slaves

SCENERY, COSTUMES, AND PROPS

- *Mitzrayim* backdrop

- "Princely" clothing for Mosheh in Egypt

- Tattered clothing for slaves

- Large bricks or blocks for slaves to carry

- Cloth or towel (to go around the waist), head covering, and whip (long ribbon) for the Egyptian taskmaster

- Robe and sandals, sneakers, or shoes for Mosheh in Midian

- Shepherd's staff/rod (yardstick or empty wrapping paper roll)

- A rubber or toy snake

- Sheep

- Burning bush (large plant with sparkling tinsel or tissue paper to look like fire)

SUGGESTED SCENE AND NARRATION

Against the backdrop of *Mitzrayim*, Mosheh is watching as the Egyptian taskmasters stand guard over the Jewish slaves, who are making bricks.

Narrator: Mosheh has been nursed by his birth mother, Yocheved, and is now a prince in *Paroh*'s palace with his mother, the daughter of *Paroh*. He has not lived the life of a slave. One day he is walking outside the palace and is watching the way the Jewish slaves are treated by the Egyptian taskmasters.

Taskmaster: Slaves! Work harder! Build these bricks faster!

Narrator: A taskmaster whips one of the slaves to make him work harder.

Slave: I'm working as hard as I can!

Taskmaster: You need to work harder!

Narrator: The Egyptian whips the slave again, and the slave falls down.

Mosheh: Stop beating that slave!

Narrator: Mosheh hits the taskmaster. The taskmaster falls over and dies.

Mosheh: Oh no! If *Paroh* finds out about this, I'll be killed. I must run away. *(Mosheh runs away.)*

(Place the bush against the backdrop, place sheep near the bush. Mosheh is holding his rod [stick] and wearing sandals/sneakers.)

Narrator: Mosheh runs away to the land of Midian. He stays in Midian and marries a woman named Tziporah. Mosheh spends his time as a shepherd. *(Mosheh is holding his staff, watching the sheep.)* One day, Mosheh is tending a flock of sheep. The sheep wander into the wilderness, and Mosheh follows. *(He turns to look at the bush.)*

Mosheh: What is this? I must turn and look at this marvelous sight. This bush is on fire, but it's not burning up! Why doesn't the bush burn up?

Narrator: When God sees that Mosheh has turned to look, God calls to him out of the bush.

God: Mosheh, Mosheh.

Mosheh:	Here I am.
God:	Do not come closer. Take your sandals off your feet because the place on which you are standing is holy ground.
Narrator:	Mosheh takes off his sandals.
God:	I am the God of your father, the God of Avraham, the God of Yitzchak, and the God of Yaakov.
Narrator:	Mosheh hides his face because he is afraid to look at God.
God:	I have seen the struggle of My people in *Mitzrayim*. I hear their cries because the Egyptian taskmasters make them work so hard in the hot sun. I know they are suffering. I have come down to rescue them from the Egyptians and bring them to a beautiful land, a land flowing with milk and honey. It is the land of Canaan.
Mosheh:	Why have you chosen **me** to do this?
God:	Don't worry. I will be with you.
Mosheh:	How will I prove to *B'nei Yisrael* that God is with me? Why would they want to follow me?
God:	Mosheh, throw your rod down on the ground.
Narrator:	Mosheh's rod turns into a snake. *(Throw the rubber/toy snake on top of the rod.)* Mosheh jumps away.
God:	Now, Mosheh, pick up the snake by the tail.
Narrator:	As Mosheh picks up the snake, it turns back into a rod. *(Mosheh picks up the stick.)*
God:	This is a sign that I will be with you. When *Paroh* and *B'nei Yisarel* see this, they will listen to you.
Mosheh:	God, I'm not a very good speaker. Sometimes I can't think of the right words to say. What should I do?
God:	I will give you the right words. You may also bring your brother, Aharon, who speaks well. I will tell you what to say,

you will tell Aharon, and Aharon will speak to *Paroh* and *B'nei Yisrael.*

Mosheh: I will do as you ask.

DISCUSSION QUESTIONS

- Why do you think Mosheh had such compassion for the slaves?

- Why do you think God spoke to Mosheh through the Burning Bush?

- Why do you think Mosheh has so many excuses about why he can't do what God asks? *(He's scared.)*

- When Mosheh tells God he doesn't think he can do what God asks, how does God solve this problem?

PUPPETS

Create the following props, and add them to the puppet bag:

- A "princely" robe and a shepherd's robe for Mosheh

- Egyptian taskmaster clothes (something like a skirt)

- Mosheh's staff/rod made from a branch or a craft stick

- Crumpled green tissue paper to use as a bush

RELATED ACTIVITIES

Burning Bush

You'll need:

- 9 × 12–inch light blue construction paper

- Small, thin twigs gathered from outside (if unavailable, use craft sticks or coffee stirrers)

- Green tempera paint

- Special brush for painting grass and leaves (see page 14)

- Small pieces of "fire"-colored tissue paper, cut or torn

- Gold glitter

- Cotton balls

- White paper

- Markers

- Scissors

- Glue

1. Give each child a piece of construction paper, placing horizontally.

2. Children will take several small twigs and glue them to the paper to form a bush.

3. Using the green paint and paintbrush, create leaves for the bush and grass for the ground.

4. Put several dots of glue on the bush. Add crumpled tissue paper for flames.

5. On the white paper, children will draw a picture of Mosheh. Cut out the picture, and glue Mosheh near the bush. Put a stick in his hand for his staff/rod.

6. Using cotton balls, create one or more sheep. Children may also create clouds for the sky. Embellish with markers.

7. Drizzle a little glue over the bush and shake on some glitter. As an alternative to gluing the bush and Mosheh flat, you may lay the paper on the table and affix the bush and Mosheh standing on the paper.

WALL TORAH

You may want to create two different murals for this chapter. Both will be described.

Mosheh and the Slaves

Invite the children to fashion artistic representations of:

- Slaves building bricks (made from sand—put glue on the paper and sprinkle with sand)

- Mosheh in "princely" clothing

- Egyptian taskmasters

- Sun

Mosheh and the Burning Bush

Children may fashion artistic representations of:

- Burning Bush

- Mosheh as a shepherd with a staff

- Sheep

- Mountainous background

- Sun

One day, while chasing a sheep, Moshe talks to God through the burning bush. God tells Moshe to ask Paroah, "Let my people go!"

LESSON 28

Moses and Pharaoh / The Ten Plagues

עֶשֶׂר הַמַּכּוֹת

Eser HaMakot

Exodus 7:14–12:42

INTRODUCTION

Mosheh leaves Midian and returns to *Mitzrayim* with his family. He meets Aharon and tells him about his encounter with God. Mosheh and Aharon talk to *B'nei Yisrael,* and they are relieved that God has noticed their suffering. However, *Paroh* is not as receptive to Mosheh and Aharon. In response to their plea, *Paroh* increases the workload of the slaves, making their lives even more miserable. God assures Mosheh that *Paroh* will let *B'nei Yisrael* go when *Paroh* realizes the power of the God of the Jews. Each time *Paroh* refuses to let the Jews go free, a terrible plague is brought upon the land, which affects only the Egyptians. After the last of the *Eser Makot* (עֶשֶׂר מַכּוֹת), the Ten Plagues, *Paroh* changes his mind.

SYNOPSIS

Mosheh and Aharon plead with *Paroh* as God commands, saying, "The God of the Jewish people sent us here to tell you, 'Let My people go so they may worship Me!'" When *Paroh* does not respond, Aharon touches his rod to the Nile River, and the water turns to blood. The Egyptians can no longer drink the water. After seven days, Mosheh and Aharon once again plead with *Paroh*. This time, when *Paroh* refuses, the land is covered with frogs. Mosheh and Aharon continue to plead with *Paroh*. Each time *Paroh* refuses, another plague is brought upon the Egyptians. Next, there is the plague of lice, followed by swarms of insects, then wild beasts, followed by a disease that kills the cattle. Then there are boils (painful bumps on people's bodies), then terrible hail, and then locusts that eat up all the plants and crops. The ninth plague causes several days of darkness. After *Paroh* can no longer put up with each of the plagues, he agrees to let *B'nei Yisrael* go free. Then, just as they're about to leave, *Paroh* changes his mind. Finally, Mosheh warns *Paroh* that the tenth plague will be the worst of all: the firstborn of every Egyptian family shall die.

In preparation for the tenth plague, Mosheh instructs *B'nei Yisrael* to kill a lamb and put some of the blood on the doorposts (frame around the door) of each house occupied by a Jewish family. The blood will let the Angel of Death know to **pass over** the homes of *B'nei Yisrael* on the night of the tenth plague so no Jews will die. In the middle of this terrible night, *Paroh* calls for Mosheh and Aharon and says to them, "Go! Leave *Mitzrayim*! Take everything with you including your animals! You are free to worship your God the way you want!" *B'nei Yisrael* leaves in such a hurry, they pack their dough before it has time to rise to bake it into bread. After this night, God asks *B'nei Yisrael* to remember this forever, by celebrating this event, Passover (Pesach), for seven days each year. During these seven days, Jews will eat unleavened (flat) bread, matzah (מַצָּה), to remember the bread that was not able to rise.

The next lesson is a continuation of the story presented in this lesson, using the same costumes and a few additional props. They may easily be combined, creating a longer lesson, if you wish.

CAST

- Mosheh

- Aharon

- *Paroh*

- *B'nei Yisrael*

SCENERY, COSTUMES, AND PROPS

- *Mitzrayim* backdrop

- Epyptian royal clothing for *Paroh*

- Throne for *Paroh*

- Desert robes and a staff for Mosheh

- Desert robes for Aharon

- Desert robes for *B'nei Yirael*

- An assortment of "plagues" (see page 214)

SUGGESTED SCENE AND NARRATION

The scene begins with *Paroh* sitting on his throne against the background of *Mitzrayim*.

Narrator: Mosheh and Aharon go to *Paroh* to plead with him as God commands.

Aharon: The God of the Jewish people sent us here to tell you, "Let My people go so they may worship Me!"

Narrator: *Paroh* does not answer. He sits on his throne with a mean face.

Aharon: If you don't let the Jewish people go, God will cause terrible things to happen.

Paroh: I don't care! You don't scare me!

Aharon: Watch what happens when I touch my rod to the Nile River.

Narrator: As Aharon touches his rod to the river, the water turns to blood.

Aharon: Let's see how the people of Egypt feel when they can no longer drink the water.

Narrator: After seven days, Mosheh and Aharon once again plead with *Paroh*.

Aharon and Mosheh: God says, "Let My people go!"

Paroh: I will **not** let them go!

Narrator: This time, when he refuses, the land is covered with frogs. Mosheh and Aharon continue to plead with *Paroh*. Each time *Paroh* refuses, another plague is brought upon the Egyptians. Next there is lice, followed by swarms of insects, then a disease that kills the cattle, then boils (painful bumps on people's bodies), then terrible hail, and then locusts that eat up all the plants and crops.

• • • • • • • • •   *Torah Alive!*

Aharon: *Paroh*, if you do not let the slaves go free, there will be several days of darkness. The Egyptians will be very unhappy.

Narrator: Finally, *Paroh* and the Egyptians can no longer put up with the plagues, and *Paroh* calls Mosheh and Aharon to the palace.

Paroh: Take your slaves and leave.

Mosheh: Aharon, we must tell *B'nei Yisrael* to get ready to leave.

Paroh: Wait! I've changed my mind. You may **not** leave!

Mosheh: *Paroh*, I'm warning you. The tenth plague will be the worst of all. The firstborn of every Egyptian family shall die!

Paroh: You don't scare me. Your people may **not** leave. Now, go away!

Narrator: Mosheh must now talk to *B'nei Yisrael* to tell them how to protect themselves against the tenth plague.

Mosheh: *B'nei Yisrael*, you need to kill a lamb and put some of the blood on the doorposts [frame around the door] of each of your houses. The blood will let the Angel of Death know to pass over your homes at night so no Jews will die.

Narrator: The night of the tenth plague is a terrible and sad night. Even *Paroh* is very sad. Finally, in the middle of this terrible night, *Paroh* calls for Mosheh and Aharon.

Paroh: Go! Leave *Mitzrayim*! Take everything with you including your animals! You are free to worship your God the way you want!

Mosheh: *B'nei Yisrael*, pack quickly! *Paroh* has agreed to let the Jewish people leave *Mitzrayim*!

Narrator: *B'nei Yisrael* leave in such a hurry, they pack their dough before it has time to rise to bake it into bread. After this terrible night, God asks *B'nei Yisrael* to remember this forever, by celebrating this event, Passover (Pesach), for seven days each year. During these seven days, Jews will eat unleavened bread, matzah, to remember the bread that was not able to rise.

DISCUSSION QUESTIONS

• Why do you think *Paroh* did not want the slaves to leave *Mitzrayim*?

• What finally convinced *Paroh* to let the slaves go free?

• What do we call the flat, unleavened bread we eat to remind us of *B'nei Yisrael* leaving *Mitzrayim* in a hurry?

• Why does God want us to have a celebration each year to remember the time the Jews were slaves and then became free?

PUPPETS

Create the following props, and add them to the puppet bags:

• Egyptian royal clothing for *Paroh*

• Desert clothing for Aharon

The "Plagues of *Mitzrayim*" (see page 214) can also be used with the puppets.

RELATED ACTIVITIES

Make Matzah

This is a great time of year to compare bread that rises (leavened bread) with bread that doesn't rise (unleavened bread or matzah). You might plan this activity for a Thursday and Friday. On Thursday, make your favorite recipe for challah dough. Make enough dough for one class challah and a personal challah for each child. During the process, show the children how the yeast "grows" when combined with the water. The yeast will bring air into the dough, and the children will observe the dough rising. Place the covered dough in the refrigerator overnight. It will continue to rise slowly.

On Friday morning, punch down the challah dough, and give each child a piece of dough about the size of an orange. The children will shape the dough into a personal challah. Be creative with the shapes! As the challah rises again, make matzah using the recipe that follows. Use the class challah for Shabbat preparations in your class. Have children taste the matzah. Children will bring their challah home to share with their families and treat them to a taste of matzah!

Matzah

You'll need:

- A large bowl
- Rolling pins
- Measuring cups
- Forks
- Flour or Passover cake flour
- Water

1. Set oven on highest temperature setting.
2. Measure 1 part water and 3 parts flour.
3. Mix and knead into a firm ball of 1–2 inches.
4. Roll out dough as thin as possible.
5. Poke holes in the dough with the forks.
6. Bake on the oven racks for 2–3 minutes until done.
7. Remove and lay flat.
8. The matzah is rather bland in taste, but it's a fun experience!

Plagues of *Mitzrayim*

Create "plagues" to use as props for the narration or with the puppets.

Place each "plague" in a container. Place containers on a table or corner of the room decorated as *Mitzrayim*.

- Blood: a few drops of red food coloring added to a plastic bottle filled with water.

- Frogs: jumping frogs from a party catalog or dollar store

- Lice: little plastic bugs from a party catalog or dollar store

- Wild beasts: hand puppets or toy figures of wild animals

- Cattle disease: toy cows turned upside down

- Boils: bubble wrap

- Hail: styrofoam popcorn packing material

- Locusts: big plastic bugs from dollar store or party catalog

- Darkness: sunglasses

- Death of the firstborn: baby dolls

WALL TORAH

Eek! The Ten Plagues!

Cut ten pieces of white paper to fit in the allotted space for the mural. Divide the children into ten groups. Invite each group to choose a plague to illustrate, and encourage them to choose their own art medium to fashion their pictures. Attach the pictures to the mural paper in the order of the Ten Plagues.

LESSON 29

Leaving Egypt / Miriam and the Women

יְצִיאַת מִצְרַיִם / מִרְיָם

Y'tziat Mitzrayim / Miryam

Exodus 13:17–15:21

INTRODUCTION

There is perhaps no other event in Jewish history that holds such importance, excitement, and enduring meaning as *Y'tziat Mitzrayim* (יְצִיאַת מִצְרַיִם), the Exodus from Egypt. Because of its importance, we are reminded of the Exodus by making constant reference to this event in our daily prayers and in the *Kiddush* over the wine on Friday evening. Metaphorically speaking, all Jews were present at the Exodus, and subsequently at Mount Sinai.

SYNOPSIS

Through God's guidance and Mosheh's leadership, *B'nei Yisrael* flee from their homes in the middle of that frightful night, hoping that *Paroh* will not change his mind yet again, as they come to the shores of *Yam Suf* (יַם סוּף), the Reed Sea. However, when *Paroh* finds out that *B'nei Yisrael* have actually left, he can't believe he has lost his force of slaves, and he sends his soldiers on chariots to go after them. As *B'nei Yisrael* see the chariots approaching, they cry out to God and Mosheh. Mosheh tells *B'nei Yisrael*, "Have no fear! Watch the wonders God will perform to deliver us from slavery today." Then God tells Mosheh, "Lift up your rod and hold your arm over the sea and split it so *B'nei Yisrael* may walk through on dry ground." As Mosheh holds his arm over the sea, the waters separate and form a wall on either side of the dry land so *B'nei Yisrael* is able to walk through. As they reach the other side, they see the Egyptian soldiers coming close. God tells Mosheh, "Hold out your arm over the sea so the waters may come down on the Egyptian soldiers and their chariots." Mosheh does as God tells him, and *Paroh*'s army is swallowed up in the sea. When *B'nei Yisrael* see the wondrous power of God, they have faith in God and Mosheh. Then Miryam (מִרְיָם), the sister of Mosheh and Aharon, and all the women, take tambourines in their hands and dance in praise of God while Mosheh recites a song of celebration.

CAST

- *Paroh*

- Mosheh

- Miryam

- *B'nei Yisrael*

- Egyptian guards and soldiers

SCENERY, COSTUMES, AND PROPS

- *Mitzrayim* backdrop

- Robes and head coverings for *B'nei Yisrael*, including Mosheh and Miryam

- Tambourines

- Large sheet or cheesecloth for the "sea"

- Egyptian garb for Egyptian guards and soldiers

- Egyptian royal clothing for *Paroh*

SUGGESTED SCENE AND NARRATION

This lesson requires two scenes. One scene will be at *Paroh*'s palace. The other will be at *Yam Suf,* the Reed Sea. *Paroh* is sitting on his throne with guards and soldiers nearby. *B'nei Yisrael* are at the shores of *Yam Suf.* Place the cloth/sheet on the floor, with adults holding either side.

Narrator:	Through God's guidance and Mosheh's leadership, *B'nei Yisrael* flee from their homes in the middle of that frightful night, hoping that *Paroh* will not change his mind yet again, as they come to the shores of the *Yam Suf.* However, when *Paroh* finds out that *B'nei Yisrael* have actually left, he can't believe he has lost his force of slaves.
Paroh:	Guards! My slaves have left! What will I do? Go and gather my soldiers with their chariots! Tell the soldiers to go after the Jews!
Narrator:	As *B'nei Yisrael* see the chariots approaching, they cry out to God and Mosheh.
B'nei Yisrael:	Mosheh! Look! *Paroh's* soldiers have come after us!

Mosheh:	Have no fear! Watch the wonders God will perform to deliver us from slavery today.
God:	Mosheh, lift up your rod and hold your arm over the sea and split it, so *B'nei Yisrael* may walk through on dry ground.
Narrator:	As Mosheh holds his arm over the sea, the waters separate and form a wall on either side of the dry land so *B'nei Yisrael* are able to walk through. (*Lift up the "sea," and have the children walk under it to the other side.*)
B'nei Yisrael:	Look, the Egyptian soldiers are coming close! They're following us through the sea!
God:	Mosheh, hold out your arm over the sea so the waters may come down on the Egyptian soldiers and their chariots.
Narrator:	Mosheh does as God tells him, and *Paroh*'s army is swallowed up in the sea. When *B'nei Yisrael* see the wondrous power of God, they have faith in God and Mosheh.
Miryam:	God has saved us from the Egyptians! This has been a miracle! Women, take your tambourines. Let's dance in thanks and praise of God.

(Play a Miryam song of your choice or play "Miriam's Song" from *And You Shall Be a Blessing* by Debbie Friedman. Invite the children to dance creatively with tambourines. Undoubtedly, the original Miryam dance was a spontaneous creation. Anything goes!)

DISCUSSION QUESTIONS

• Why do you think *Paroh* broke his promise to let *B'nei Yisrael* leave *Mitzrayim*?

• What is a miracle? Have you ever seen a miracle? (*A miracle is when something happens that can't be explained logically. It is an event that must have required God's help.*)

- What miracles happened before and after *B'nei Yisrael* left *Mitzrayim*? (*Plagues, parting of the sea, safe deliverance of* B'nei Yisrael.)

- Why did *B'nei Yisrael* celebrate after they crossed the Reed Sea?

PUPPETS

It's time to dance! Add a tambourine to the puppet bag. Cut a circle from tagboard, 1 inch in diameter, and affix several small round sequins around the perimeter.

RELATED ACTIVITIES

Parting of the Reed Sea

You'll need:

- Tempera paint in the following colors: blue, green, purple, white

- Sponge pieces cut in squares, approximately 1 inch

- Brown 9 × 12–inch construction paper

- White copy paper

- Markers

1. Prepare containers of paints. Create different shades of each color by adding varying amounts of white or combining colors. Placing paints in a dish with several sections is helpful. Place a sponge in each color.

2. Children may use the sponges to quickly dab each color on the white paper, overlapping colors. Allow paper to dry.

3. Position brown paper vertically. This will be "dry land." Draw *B'nei Yisrael* walking across the dry land.

4. Position the "water" paper over the "dry land." Staple the two papers together on the corners.

5. Children will **carefully** place scissors between the two papers and cut a wiggly line down the center of the white paper.

6. As they separate the painted white paper, they will see *B'nei Yisrael* walking across the dry land!

Tambourines

You'll need for each student:

- Two pie tins

- Four short pipe cleaners, cut in half

- Eight bells

- A button

1. Punch eight evenly spaced holes in the rim of each pie tin.

2. With pie tins facing each other, tie them together with one short piece of pipe cleaner.

3. Add a bell to the pipe cleaner and twist closed.

4. Before closing the last hole, put the button in the space between the two pie tins. This will add extra rhythmical sounds.

5. Optional: Children may decorate tambourines with permanent marker, acrylic paint, or stickers.

Create a Miryam Dance

Using "Miriam's Song" by Debbie Friedman or another favorite, invite the children to create a celebration dance using tambourines. The children will get inspiration for particular movements and choreography as they listen to the words of the song.

WALL TORAH

It will be fun depicting the parting of the Reed Sea using the painting technique described on page 221. Each child may draw a picture of him/herself crossing through the Reed Sea. Throughout history, Jews have thought of themselves as having personally been present at this miraculous liberation from slavery.

LESSON 30

Mount Sinai / The Ten Commandments

עֲשֶׂרֶת הַדִּבְּרוֹת
Aseret HaDibrot

Exodus 19:1–20:18

INTRODUCTION

Finally free from *Paroh* and the Egyptians, *B'nei Yisrael* set out on their journey to the Promised Land. Little do they know that it will be forty years until the next generation is ready to enter the Promised Land.

Depending on the school and Jewish calendars, the teacher may want to present this lesson to coincide with preparations for the holiday of Shavuot, when we celebrate the receiving of the Ten Commandments (עֲשֶׂרֶת הַדִּבְּרוֹת).

This lesson will be the conclusion of this cycle of Torah study for your students. You may plan a *siyum* (see pages 18–19) to celebrate this accomplishment. Remind your students that this is only the beginning of their lifelong study of Torah.

SYNOPSIS

Three months after they leave *Mitzrayim*, *B'nei Yisrael* enter the wilderness of Sinai. They set up camp at the bottom of the mountain. Mosheh climbs up the mountain to God, and God calls to him from the mountain. God tells Mosheh to tell *B'nei Yisrael*, "You have seen what I did to the Egyptians and how I brought you to Me. Now, if you will listen carefully to Me and follow My commandments, you will be My treasured people." Mosheh speaks these words to *B'nei Yisrael,* and they answer, "All that God has said, we will do." Mosheh brings *B'nei Yisrael*'s words back to God. God tells Mosheh, "I will come to you in a thick cloud so all the people will hear when I speak with you, and then they will trust you forever." Mosheh brings the people to the bottom of the mountain to meet God. The mountain shakes and smoke surrounds the top. God asks Mosheh to come up the mountain. These are the words that God says:

1. I am *Adonai* your God who brought you out of the land of Egypt, out of slavery.

2. You will not pray to any other god but Me. You will not make idols. You will not bow down to idols.

3. Do not ask God to do something bad to someone else.

4. Remember Shabbat and keep it holy. You may work for six days and do all your work, but on the seventh day you must rest.

5. Honor (listen to) your father and your mother.

6. Do not murder (kill).

7. Do not commit adultery.

8. Do not steal.

9. Do not lie.

10. Do not be jealous of something your neighbor or friend has.

B'nei Yisrael learn to live by these rules as they continue their journey to the Promised Land.

CAST

- Mosheh

- *B'nei Yisrael*

SCENERY, COSTUMES, AND PROPS

- A new mountainous, desert backdrop (not Canaan, not *Mitzrayim*)

- A-frame climbing equipment covered with a large cloth to look like a mountain

- Desert garb for Mosheh and *B'nei Yisrael*

- Ten Commandments cut from 12 × 18–inch tagboard. Fold paper in half vertically, and round the top corners. Open, and write numbers and Hebrew letters on the "tablets."

- Gray or black fabric or streamers for "smoke"

SUGGESTED SCENE AND NARRATION

The scene begins with all of the children, *B'nei Yisrael*, assembled around the base of the mountain.

Narrator: Three months have passed since *B'nei Yisrael* have left *Mitzrayim*. They have entered the wilderness of Sinai. They set up camp at the bottom of the mountain.

God:	Mosheh, I would like you to climb this mountain and come talk with Me.
Mosheh:	I will do as You ask. (Mosheh climbs the mountain/ladder.)
Narrator:	Mosheh climbs up the mountain to God, and God calls to him from the mountain.
God:	Mosheh, tell *B'nei Yisrael* My words, the words of God. These are My words: "You have seen the miracles that I have performed. Now, if you will listen carefully to Me and follow My commandments, you will be My treasured people."
Mosheh:	I spoke with God, and you have heard God's words. What shall I tell God?
Narrator:	*B'nei Yisrael* answered, saying, "All that God has said, we will do."
Mosheh:	God, *B'nei Yisrael* has said, "All that God has said, we will do."
God:	Mosheh, I will come to you in a thick cloud so all the people will hear when I speak with you, and then they will trust you forever.
Mosheh:	*B'nei Yisrael*, you need to come to the bottom of the mountain to meet God.
Narrator:	The mountain shakes and smoke surrounds the top. *(Shake the "mountain" and wave a gray/black fabric or streamers over the top.)*
God:	Mosheh, come up the mountain so I may speak to you, and then you will give My words to *B'nei Yisrael*.
Narrator:	Mosheh climbs up the mountain and receives the Ten Commandments.
Mosheh:	These are the words that God says:

1. I am *Adonai* your God who brought you out of the land of Egypt, out of slavery.

2. You will not pray to any other god but Me. You will not make idols. You will not bow down to idols.

3. Do not ask God to do something bad to someone else.

4. Remember Shabbat and keep it holy. You may work for six days and do all your work, but on the seventh day you must rest.

5. Honor (listen to) you father and your mother.

6. Do not murder (kill).

7. Do not commit adultery. (When you are married, you can't have another boyfriend or girlfriend.)

8. Do not steal.

9. Do not lie.

10. Do not be jealous of something your neighbor or friend has.

Narrator: *B'nei Yisrael* learn to live by these rules as they continue their journey to the Promised Land.

DISCUSSION QUESTIONS

- What's another word for commandments? *(Rules)*

- If we didn't have rules, what would happen?

- Which of the commandments talk about a person's relationship (connection) with God?

- Which of the commandments talk about how a person treats members of his or her family?

- Which of the commandments talk about how people treat other people?

- If you could add an eleventh commandment, what would it be?

PUPPETS

Create the following props, and add them to the puppet bag:

- Shape of the Ten Commandments cut from tagbord to use as a prop for Mosheh

- A cloth to cover a small chair to use as Mount Sinai.

RELATED ACTIVITIES

Mosheh and Mount Sinai

You'll need for each child:

- 9 × 12–inch light blue construction paper

- A 4 × 2–inch rectangle of white construction paper

- Craft stick

- Sand

- Glue with brush

- Markers

1. Holding the blue paper vertically, children may draw a large mountain, Mount Sinai, leaving about 2 inches free at the top.

2. Draw as many people, *B'nei Yisrael,* as desired at the base of the mountain.

3. Paint the mountain with glue. Apply sand.

4. Illustrate Mosheh holding the Ten Commandments on the white rectangle. Cut out and affix it to the craft stick.

5. Cut a horizontal slit toward the top of the mountain.

6. Children will hold Mosheh behind the picture and watch him climb to the top of Mount Sinai as they push him throught the slit.

WALL TORAH

After drawing a large mountain, Mount Sinai, on the mural paper, children may draw a picture of Mosheh holding the Ten Commandments on the top of the mountain. Each child may draw a picture of him/herself at the base of Mount Sinai. Throughout history, Jews have thought of themselves as having personally been present at this awesome event.

This is the last picture in the Wall Torah. This picture should be next to the second *eitz chayim. Mazal Tov!*

Appendix A
Dance Instructions

Abbreviations:

R	Right	CW	Clockwise	
L	Left	CCW	Counterclockwise	
Fwd	Forward	×	times	
Bkwd	Backward			

There are many sources of appropriate music for these dances, including *The Real Complete Jewish Party Music Collection* by David & Gila's Band, Success Records 8367.

HATZIPORIM (ISRAELI BIRD DANCE)

Formation: Children in partners scattered around the room. Children face their partners.

Counts   Movements

PART ONE

1–4	With both hands, make a beak shape and snap the "beak" 4×
5–8	With bent elbows, flap arms like a bird 4×
9–12	Bend knees and wiggle hips 4×
13–16	Clap hands 4×
17–64	Repeat 1–16 three more times

PART TWO

1–16	Hook R elbows with partner, turn CW with 16 skips
17–32	Hook L elbows with partner, turn CCW with 16 skips

YEISH LANU TAYISH
(WE HAVE A BILLY GOAT)

Formation: Form two lines facing each other. Couples stand opposite one another, forming an aisle or space between them.

Note: These instructions may sound complicated, but this traditional Israeli folk dance is actually quite simple and exciting. Once the dance has been taught and mastered, the children will enjoy it for many years to come. It would be helpful to position one teacher at the front of the line and one at the end.

Counts	Movements
1–8	Head (first) couple joins hands and slides down the aisle. Everyone else claps.
9–16	Repeat 1–8, sliding back to place
17–40	The head couple "casts off." Everyone faces the front of the room in two lines, one child behind the other. All walk forward, following the head couple, which leads the two lines away from each other. Members of each line follow their own head couple. The head couple leads the line to the spot where the last couple was standing. It may be helpful to form a "train," with each child's arms on the shoulders of the person ahead of him or her. The head couple forms a bridge at the end of the line. (You may mark this spot on the floor with tape.) Each child passes the bridge, then turns to go under the bridge, meeting his or her partner. Each child joins his or her partner's

hand as they go under the bridge, walking forward to the front of the room. There is now a new head couple! The former head couple is now at the end of the line.

LA RASPA (MEXICAN HAT DANCE)

Formation: Children in partners scattered around the room. Children face their partners.

Counts	Movements
PART ONE	Hands on own waist. Start with one heel fwd.
1	Switch heels
2–3	Switch heels 2x
4	Clap 2x
5–32	Repeat 1–4 (7x)
PART TWO	Link R elbows with partner, L arm up
1–8	Walk around 8 steps with partner, CW
9–16	Switch arms and directions; walk around 8 steps CCW

(Note: Some recordings allow for 16 steps in each direction)

RAMAYA (AFRICAN LINE DANCE)

Formation: Lines facing front.

Counts   Movements

PART ONE

Counts	Movements
1–2	Kick R foot fwd (2×) while hopping on L
3–4	RLR in place
5–8	Reverse 1–4
9–32	Repeat 1–8 (3×)

PART TWO

Counts	Movements
1–2	R to R, close L to R (hands move like windshield wipers)
3–6	Repeat 1–2 (3x)
7–8	RLR in place
9–16	Reverse 1–8
17–32	Repeat 1–16

PART THREE

Counts	Movements
1–12	3 R and L cha-cha steps turning in a circle to R in place (R cha-cha step: R, L, R, pause; L cha-cha step: L, R, L, pause). Use arms, bending one fwd and one behind bkwd. Switch arms with each step.
13	Bend down and touch floor
14	Slap thighs
15	Clap
16	Throw arms in air, jump in place, scream "Hey!"

Appendix B
Recipe for Cookie Dough

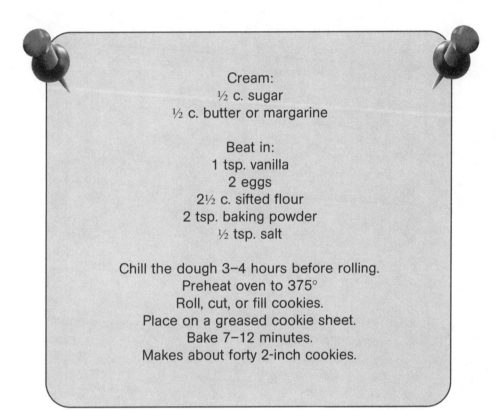

Cream:
½ c. sugar
½ c. butter or margarine

Beat in:
1 tsp. vanilla
2 eggs
2½ c. sifted flour
2 tsp. baking powder
½ tsp. salt

Chill the dough 3–4 hours before rolling.
Preheat oven to 375°
Roll, cut, or fill cookies.
Place on a greased cookie sheet.
Bake 7–12 minutes.
Makes about forty 2-inch cookies.

Appendix C
Sample Letter to Parents

(Date)

Dear Parents,

In class, we are involved in studies and activities from Lesson _____ of *Torah Alive!* We invite you to join our studies, in your home, by reading the designated pages for this lesson and exploring the related dicussion questions and activities in *Torah Alive! Parent Connection.* Feel free to share with the class special insights or projects you enjoyed with your family.

Shalom,

(The Teachers)

Appendix D
Useful Web Sites

www.urj.org/educate/ganeinu/index.shtml

The Union of Reform Judaism offers this online bulletin, *Ganeinu—Our Garden*. This publication addresses educational issues that concern Jewish early childhood programs. It offers discussion and insight to assist directors, teachers, and parents with the daily challenges of educating in early childhood.

www.urj.org/educate/childhood.shtml

The early childhood section of the URJ's Department of Lifelong Jewish Learning Web site includes resources and educational activities for the home and classroom. This site also includes parents' resources.

www.bjeny.org/434.asp?dept=Early%20Childhood&Programs_ID=111

This page from the Web site of the Board of Jewish Education of New York gives information about New York BJE's history with early childhood education, a description of its programs, and instructions for how to become a member to access the BJE's resources.

www.kididdles.com/shop2/itm01972.htm

This is a for-profit site, offering for sale a variety of early childhood books, music, videos, and software. A site search using the word "Jewish" will yield many results.

www.jesna.org/cgi-bin/ilive.php3?op1=earlyc

The Jewish Education Service of North America (JESNA) is a non-denominational, Federation-based Jewish educational organization. It helps coordinate, plan, and develop Jewish educational initiatives throughout North America.

This section of JESNA's site offers an article about how to most effectively integrate Israel education into the early childhood classroom. The article discusses some of the challenges of much current practice, as well as suggestions for strengthening students' Israel learning.

Another section of JESNA's Web site (**www.jesna.org/cgi-bin/earlychild. php3**) includes early childhood education discussion groups, professional development programs, and an "electronic toolkit."

www.jafi.org.il/education/child/

Produced by The Early Childhood Division of the Jewish Agency for Israel and its Department for Jewish Zionist Education, this site offers a variety of resources: activities, curricula, and children's books (and their teacher's guides) for downloading; professional exchange opportunities; and projects, articles, and information on Jewish early childhood education. The site focuses on Israel education both inside and outside of Israel.

www.bjesf.org/ECEhome.html

The non-denominational Bureau of Jewish Education of San Francisco offers this useful site. It includes articles, information, Jewish texts, and terms for the educator's use. It also contains a discussion section for ECE professionals and a section serving the needs of the classroom. Each month's resources cover a new theme, such as a Jewish holiday or concept, and site visitors can access previous months' resources.

www.angelfire.com/fl/ajl/rainbowfish/presentation.html

Heidi Estrin, librarian at Feldman Children's Library of Congregation B'nai Israel in Boca Raton, FL, offers material at this site that she presented at the annual convention of the Association of Jewish Libraries. She presents a bibliography of secular children's books that highlight Jewish values. The site is conveniently arranged by value.

www.j.co.il/

This useful Web site contains a variety of practical Jewish learning resources and tools. The site includes a Hebrew sign-maker, a Jewish wisdom database, games, and clipart.

www.virtualjerusalem.com/

The bottom of this site's home page contains links to Jewish resources. These include stories, crafts, and a recipe archive.

groups.yahoo.com/group/cajeearlychildhood/

This is the Jewish early childhood educators' listserv from the Coalition for the Advancement of Jewish Education (CAJE). CAJE, the largest non-denominational organization of Jewish educators in North America, works to improve educators' and institutions' pedagogic and Judaic skills and the culture of Jewish education throughout North America.

groups.yahoo.com/group/jewishreggio

This listserv brings together a group of Jewish early childhood educators interested in creating and perfecting Reggio-inspired classrooms that effectively integrate secular subject matter with Jewish content, values, and Hebrew vocabulary.

www.jewishlife.org/pdf/autumn_2002.pdf

The Autumn 2002 issue of *Contact: The Journal of Jewish Life Network* focuses on Jewish early childhood education. The Jewish Life Network (also called the Steinhardt Foundation) is a philanthropic organization that aims to renew and revitalize Jewish life through educational, religious, and cultural endeavors.

www.meltonarts.org/artedu_lessonplans.php

MeltonArts is a project of the Melton Coalition for Creative Interaction. This coalition aims to promote Jewish learning through the arts. This section of the MeltonArts Web site includes lesson plans for teaching Judaism through art. To find lessons specifically geared toward early childhood settings, use the site's search engine to find "early childhood."

www.adl.org/education/miller/miller_printable.asp

This site contains a description of the Miller Early Childhood Initiative of A WORLD OF DIFFERENCE Institute—a project of the Anti-Defamation League. Aside from information about early childhood educator workshops, the site also lists some ways that educators can help students learn about diversity and coexistence skills. The Anti-Defamation League was established over ninety years ago in response to anti-Semitism in America. Now an organization that works against hatred and bigotry in all American communities, the ADL sponsors A WORLD OF DIFFERENCE Institute to help educate students and teachers for a diverse society.

jcca.org

This Web site is the electronic home of the national, non-denominational Jewish Community Center Association. The site houses JCCA's Early Childhood Education department, which features a theme-based preschool curriculum that follows the structure of the Hebrew calendar.

www.geocities.com/amynealw

A Jewish early childhood educator created this site to be an online community and source of resources for her and her colleagues. The site includes resource reviews, activities, ideas, and discussion groups.

www.torahtots.com

This colorful, fun site offers an Orthodox perspective on holidays and Torah texts. Based on a traveling children's performance, it features games, activities, coloring pages, holiday texts, and "Parsha on Parade," which includes a description of the week's Torah portion using a wide array of Torah-related Hebrew words.

Glossary of Hebrew Terms

Term	Hebrew	English
Adam	אָדָם	Adam
adamah	אֲדָמָה	earth
Aharon	אַהֲרוֹן	Aaron
akeidah	עֲקֵדָה	binding
Aron HaKodesh	אֲרוֹן הַקֹּדֶשׁ	the Holy Ark
Aseret HaDibrot	עֲשֶׂרֶת הַדִּבְּרוֹת	the Ten Commandments
Avraham	אַבְרָהָם	Abraham
Batya	בַּתְיָה	Batya/Pharoah's daughter
Bavel	בָּבֶל	Babel
b'chorah	בְּכוֹרָה	birthright
b'eir	בְּאֵר	well
Beit El	בֵּית אֵל	Beth El
beit sohar	בֵּית סֹהַר	jail
Binyamin	בִּנְיָמִן	Benjamin
B'nei Yisrael	בְּנֵי יִשְׂרָאֵל	Children of Israel
bor	בּוֹר	pit
b'rachah	בְּרָכָה	blessing
B'reishit	בְּרֵאשִׁית	Creation
Canaan	כְּנַעַן	Canaan
chalamot	חֲלוֹמוֹת	dreams
challah	חַלָּה	challah

Term	Hebrew	English
Cham	חָם	Ham
Chavah	חַוָּה	Eve
Efrayim	אֶפְרַיִם	Ephraim
Eisav	עֵשָׂו	Esau
Eitz Chayim	עֵץ חַיִּים	Tree of Life
Eitz HaDaat	עֵץ הַדַּעַת	Tree of Knowledge
Eliezer	אֱלִיעֶזֶר	Eliezer
Eretz Yisrael	אֶרֶץ יִשְׂרָאֵל	Land of Israel
eser	עֶשֶׂר	ten
Gan Eden	גַּן עֵדֶן	Garden of Eden
hachnasat orchim	הַכְנָסַת אוֹרְחִים	hospitalty
hakafah	הַקָּפָה	parade with Torah
Har Sinai	הַר סִינַי	Mount Sinai
HaSneh HaBo-eir	הַסְנֶה הַבֹּעֵר	the Burning Bush
keshet	קֶשֶׁת	rainbow
Kiddush	קִדּוּשׁ	Kiddush
k'tonet pasim	כְּתֹנֶת פַּסִים	coat of many colors
Lavan	לָבָן	Laban
Lech l'cha	לֶךְ לְךָ	Go from here!
Lei-ah	לֵאָה	Leah
Lot	לוֹט	Lot
makot	מַכּוֹת	plagues
malachim	מַלְאָכִים	angels
midrash	מִדְרָשׁ	midrash

Glossary of Hebrew Terms

Term	Hebrew	English
migdal	מִגְדָל	tower
Miryam	מִרְיָם	Miriam
Mitzrayim	מִצְרַיִם	Egypt
M'nasheh	מְנַשֶּׁה	Manasseh
Mosheh	מֹשֶׁה	Moses
Naamah	נַעֲמָה	Noah's wife
nachash	נָחָשׁ	snake
neirot	נֵרוֹת	candles
Noach	נֹחַ	Noah
ohel	אֹהֶל	tent
orchim	אוֹרְחִים	visitors
parashah	פָּרָשָׁה	chapter
Paroh	פַּרְעֹה	Pharoah
Potifar	פּוֹטִיפַר	Potifar
Racheil	רָחֵל	Rachel
rimonim	רִמּוֹנִים	Torah ornaments
Rivkah	רִבְקָה	Rebecca
Sarah	שָׂרָה	Sarah
Shabbat	שַׁבָּת	Shabbat
Shavuot	שָׁבוּעוֹת	Shavout
Shem	שֵׁם	Shem
Shimon	שִׁמְעוֹן	Simon
Simchat Torah	שִׂמְחַת תּוֹרָה	Simchat Torah
siyum	סִיּוּם	celebration
s'lichah	סְלִיחָה	forgiveness

Term	Hebrew	English
Sukkot	סֻכּוֹת	Sukkot
sulam	סֻלָּם	ladder
teivah	תֵּבָה	ark
tinok	תִּינוֹק	baby
Torah	תּוֹרָה	Torah
tzedakah	צְדָקָה	righteousness/ charity
Tziporah	צִפֹּרָה	Tziporah
Yaakov	יַעֲקֹב	Jacob
Yam Suf	יַם סוּף	Reed Sea
Yefet	יֶפֶת	Yefet
Y'hudah	יְהוּדָה	Judah
Yishmaeilim	יִשְׁמָעֵאלִים	Ishmaelites
Yisrael	יִשְׂרָאֵל	Israel
Yitzchak	יִצְחָק	Isaac
Yocheved	יוֹכֶבֶד	Yocheved
yonah	יוֹנָה	dove
Yoseif	יוֹסֵף	Joseph
y'tziah	יְצִיאָה	exodus

Glossary of Hebrew Terms

Bibliography and Resources

CREATION

Creation: Books

Fisher, Leonard Everett. *The Seven Days of Creation*. New York: Holiday House, 1981.

Greene, Rhonda Gowler. *The Beautiful World that God Made*. Grand Rapids, MI: Eerdmans Books for Young Readers, 2002.

Greengard, Alison. *In The Beginning* (Hebrew and English). Oakland, CA: EKS Publishing, 2000.

McKissack, Fredrick, and Patricia McKissack. *God Made Something Wonderful*. Minneapolis: Augsburg, 1989.

Nerlove, Miriam. *Shabbat*. Morton Grove, IL: Albert Whitman, 1998.

Ray, Jane. *The Story of Creation*. New York: Dutton Children's Books, 1992.

Reed, Allison. *Genesis, The Story of Creation*. New York: Schocken Books, 1981.

Sattgask, L. J. *When the World Was New*. Grand Rapids, MI: Zonderman, 2001.

Creation: Music

Avni, Fran. "Once Upon A Time." *The Seventh Day*. Lemonstone Records, LSCD1003.

Glaser, Sam. "The Seven Days." *Kol Bamidbar: A Musical Journey through the Five Books of Moses.* Los Angeles: Glaser Musicworks, 1999.

Kol B'seder. "In the Beginning." *Songs for Growin'.* Transcontinental Music Publications 950077.

ADAM V'CHAVAH (ADAM AND EVE)

Howard, Fern. *Adam and Eve.* Leicestershire, England: Ladybird Books, 1990.

Hutton, Warwick. *Adam and Eve: The Bible Story.* New York: Macmillan, 1987.

NOACH (NOAH)

Noach: Books

Faulkner, Paul. *Two-by-Two.* Los Angeles: Price Stern Sloan, 1993.

Fussenegger, Gertrud. *Noah's Ark.* New York: J. B. Lippincott, 1982.

Geisert, Arthur. *After the Flood.* Boston: Houghton Mifflin, 1994.

Geisert, Arthur. *The Ark.* Boston: Houghton Mifflin, 1988.

Hayward, Linda. *Noah's Ark.* New York: Random House, 1987.

Hogrogian, Nonny (Illustrator). *Noah's Ark.* New York: Alfred A. Knopf, 1986.

Hollyer, Belinda. *Noah and the Ark.* Morristown, NJ: Silver Burdett, 1984.

Hutton, Warwick. *Noah and the Great Flood.* New York: Atheneum, 1977.

Lepon, Shoshana. *Noah and the Rainbow*. New York: Judaica Press, 1993.

Le Tord, Bijou. *Noah's Trees*. New York: Harper Collins, 1999.

Lorimer, Lawrence T. *Noah's Ark*. New York: Random House, 1978.

Ray, Jane. *Noah's Ark*. New York: Dutton Children's Books, 1990.

Reid, Barbara. *Two by Two*. New York: Scholastic, 1992.

Rouss, Sylvia. *The Littlest Pair*. New York: Pitspopany Press, 2001.

Singer, Isaac Bashevis. *Why Noah Chose the Dove*. New York: Farrar, Straus & Giroux, 1973.

Spier, Peter. *Noah's Ark*. New York: Doubleday, 1977.

Noach: Music

Friedman, Debbie. "The Rainbow Blessing." *Live at the Del.* Sounds Write Productions, SWP 607.

Glaser, Sam. "Two By Two." *Kol Bamidbar: A Musical Journey through the Five Books of Moses*. Los Angeles: Sam Glaser Musicworks, 1999.

Zim, Paul. *Zimmy Zim's Zoo*. Paul Zim Productions Inc., 1994.

Noach: Books about Colors

Ehlert, Lois. *Color Zoo*. New York: Harper Collins, 1989.

Ehlert, Lois. *Planting a Rainbow*. San Diego: Harcourt Brace, 1988.

Freeman, Don. *A Rainbow of My Own*. New York: Puffin Books, 1966.

Hoban, Tana. *Colors Everywhere*. New York: Greenwillow Books, 1995.

Hoban, Tana. *Is It Red? Is It Yellow?* New York: Mulberry, 1987.

Hoban, Tana. *Of Colors and Things.* New York: Mulberry Books, 1996.

Jonas, Ann. *Color Dance.* New York: Greenwillow Books, 1989.

Lionni, Leo. *A Color of His Own.* New York: Knopf, 1997.

Lionni, Leo. *Frederick.* New York: Knopf, 1967.

Lionni, Leo. *Little Blue and Little Yellow.* New York: Mulberry Books, 1995.

McMillan, Bruce. *Growing Colors.* New York: Harper Collins, 1994.

Munsch, Robert N. *Purple, Green and Yellow.* Buffalo, NY: Firefly Books, 1992.

Walsh, Ellen Stoll. *Mouse Paint.* San Diego: Harcourt Brace, 1989.

Noach: Books about Animals

Aliki. *Milk: From Cow to Carton.* New York: Harper Collins, 1992.

Barrett, Judi. *Animals Should Definitely Not Act Like People.* New York: Aladdin Paperbacks, 1989.

Barrett, Judi. *Animals Should Definitely Not Wear Clothing.* New York: Aladdin Paperbacks, 1989.

Bateman, Robert. *Safari.* Boston: Little, Brown, 1998.

Chessen, Betsey. *Animal Homes.* New York: Scholastic, 1998.

Esbensen, Barbara Juster. *Baby Whales Drink Milk.* New York: Harper Collins, 1994.

Gibbons, Gail. *Dogs.* New York: Holiday House, 1996.

Meadows, Graham. *Cats.* Milwaukee: Gareth Stevens, 1998. (Other animal titles available.)

• • • • • • • • • • Bibliography and Resources

Willow, Diane. *At Home in the Rain Forest*. Watertown, MA: Charlesbridge, 1991.

TOWER OF BABEL

Tower of Babel: Books

Greengard, Alison. *The Tower of Babel* (Hebrew and English). Oakland, CA: EKS Publishing, 2001.

Hirsh, Marilyn. *The Tower of Babel*. New York: Holiday House, 1981.

Mayer-Skumanz, Lene. *The Tower*. n.p.: Yellow Brick Road Press, 1993.

Weisner, William. *The Tower of Babel*. New York: Viking Press, 1968.

Tower of Babel: Multicultural Books

Aardema, Verna. *Why Mosquitoes Buzz in People's Ears*. New York: Dial Books for Young Readers, 1975. (A West African tale.)

Anno, Mitsumaso. *All in a Day*. New York: Philomel Books, 1986.

Beeler, Selby B. *Throw Your Tooth on the Roof: Tooth Traditions from around the World*. Boston: Houghton Mifflin, 1998.

Brendon, Stuart. *The Children's Atlas of the World*. London: Grandreams Limited, 1993.

Brown, Marcia. *The Bun*. New York: Harcourt Brace Jovanovich, 1972. (A Russian tale.)

Chocolate, Debbi. *Kente Colors*. New York: Walker and Company, 1996.

Climo, Shirley. *The Irish Cinderlad*. New York: Harper Collins, 1996. (An Irish tale.)

Demi. *Liang and the Magic Paintbrush*. New York: Henry Holt, 1980. (An Asian tale.)

dePaola, Tomie. *The Legend of the Indian Paintbrush*. New York: G. P. Putnam's Sons, 1988. (A Native American tale.)

De Zutter, Hank. *Who Says a Dog Goes Bow-wow?* New York: Doubleday, 1993.

Ehlert, Lois. *Cuckoo*. New York: Harcourt Brace, 1997. (A Mexican tale.)

Forest, Heather. *The Woman Who Flummoxed the Fairies*. New York: Harcourt Brace Jovanovich, 1990. (A Scottish tale.)

Ginsburg, Mirra. *How the Sun Was Brought Back to the Sky*. New York: Macmillan, 1975. (A Slovenian tale.)

Hamanaka, Sheila. *All the Colors of the Earth*. New York: Morrow Junior Books, 1994.

Hofbauer, Michele Pace. *Couldn't We Make a Difference?* Bridgeport, CT: Greene Bark Press, 2000. (All children of the world working toward peace.)

Hurwitz, Johanna. *New Shoes for Silvia*. New York: Morrow Junior Books, 1993. (A Latin American story.)

Kendall, Russ. *Russian Girl*. New York: Scholastic, 1994.

King, Martin Luther, Jr. *I Have a Dream*. New York: Scholastic, 1997.

McClure, Herbert. *Children of the World Say "Good Morning."* New York: Holt, Rinehart and Winston, 1963.

Miller, J. Philip, and Sheppard M. Greene. *We All Sing with the Same Voice*. New York: HarperCollins Publishers, 2001. (Includes CD).

Montanari, Donata. *Children Around the World*. Hong Kong: Kids Can Press, 2001.

Morris, Ann. *Grandma Esther Remembers: A Jewish-American Family Story.* Brookfield, CT: Millbrook Press, 2002. (Others available in the "What Was It Like, Grandma?" series, including British American, Hispanic American, Chinese American, and Native American.)

Mosel, Arlene. *Tikki Tikki Tembo.* New York: Holt, Rinehart and Winston, 1968. (A Chinese tale.)

Polacco, Patricia. *Babushka's Doll.* New York: Simon & Schuster, 1990. (A tale of a Russian grandmother and her granddaughter.)

Simon, Norma. *All Kinds of Children.* Morton Grove, IL: Albert Whitman, 1999.

Sloat, Teri. *The Eye of the Needle.* New York: Penguin Books, 1990. (A Yupik tale.)

Snyder, Dianne. *The Boy of the Three-Year Nap.* Boston: Houghton Mifflin, 1988. (A Japanese tale.)

Spier, Peter. *People.* New York: Doubleday, 1980.

Stuve-Bodeen, Stephanie. *Elizabeti's Doll.* New York: Lee & Low Books, 1998. (A Tanzanian story.)

Surat, Michele Maria. *Angel Child, Dragon Child.* New York: Scholastic, 1983. (A Vietnamese immigrant story.)

Weiss, George (George David). *What a Wonderful World.* New York: Atheneum Books for Young Readers, 1995.

Tower of Babel: Multicultural Music

Conn Beall, Pamela, and Susan Hagen Nipp. *Wee Sing Around the World.* Los Angeles: Price Stern Sloan, 1994. (Recorded music with booklet of words and sheet music.)

Putumayo World Music: Musical adventures from many areas of the world.

Other suggested artists: Jack Grunsky, Ella Jenkins, Red Grammer.

AKEIDAT YITZCHAK—THE BINDING OF ISAAC

Cohen, Barbara. *The Binding of Isaac.* New York: Lothrop, Lee & Shepard, 1978.

YOSEIF

Yoseif: Books

Auld, Mary. *Joseph and His Brothers.* New York: Franklin Watts, 1999.

Kassirer, Sue. *Joseph and His Coat of Many Colors.* New York: Simon & Schuster Children's, 1997.

Lepon, Shoshana. *Joseph and the Dreamer.* New York: Judaica Press, 1991.

Murdock, Hy. *Joseph.* Leicestershire, England: Ladybird Books, 1985.

Pingry, Patricia. *The Story of Joseph.* Nashville: Candy Cane Press, 1998.

Williams, Marcia. *Joseph and His Magnificent Coat of Many Colors.* Cambridge, MA: Candlewick Press, 1990.

Yoseif: Music

Webber, Andrew Lloyd. *Joseph and the Amazing Technicolor Dreamcoat.* Chrysalis Records, 1982.

MOSHEH—MOSES

Mosheh: Books

Adler, David A. *A Picture Book of Passover*. New York: Holiday House, 1982.

Amery, Heather. *Moses in the Bullrushes*. London: Usborne Publishing, 1997.

Auld, Mary. *Moses in the Bullrushes*. New York: Franklin Watts, 1999.

Davies, Kate (illustrator). *Moses in the Bullrushes*. New York: Simon & Schuster Children's, 1996.

Hayward, Linda. *Baby Moses* (Step Into Reading). New York: Random House, 1989.

Hutton, Warwick. *Moses in the Bullrushes*. New York: Aladdin Books, 1986.

Lepon, Shoshana. *The Ten Plagues of Egypt*. New York: Judaica Press, 1994.

Nerlove, Miriam. *The Ten Commandments for Jewish Children*. Morton Grove, IL: Albert Whitman, 1999.

Pingry, Patricia. *The Story of Miriam and Baby Moses*. Nashville: Candy Cane Press, 2000.

Pingry, Patricia. *The Story of the Ten Commandments*. New York: Ideals Children's Books, 1989.

Topek, Susan Remick. *Ten Good Rules*. Rockville, Maryland: Kar-Ben Copies, 1991.

Mosheh: Music

Avni, Fran. *Mostly Matza*. Lemonstone Records LSCD1001.

Friedman, Debbie. *The Journey Continues*. Sounds Write Productions SWP614.

Kol B'Seder: *Songs for Growin'*. Transcontinental Music Publications 950077.

GENERAL

General: Books

Cowan, Paul. *A Torah Is Written*. New York: Jewish Publication Society, 1986.

Books Containing Stories about Jewish Values

Bogot, Howard I., and Mary K. Bogot. *Seven Animal Stories for Children*. New York: Pitspopany, 2000. (Respect, modesty, gratitude, honesty, attitude, friendship, responsibility.)

————. *Seven Animals Wag Their Tales*. New York: Pitspopany, 2000. (Helpfulness, making choices, cooperation, duty, teamwork, courage, accepting differences.)

Elkins, Dov Peretz. *Seven Delightful Stories For Every Day*. New York: Pitspopany, 2000. (Respect, modesty, gratitude, patience, hospitality, kindness, responsibility.)

Family: Books

Freedman, Florence B. *Brothers*. New York: Harper & Row, 1985.

Kalman, Bobbie. *People in My Family*. New York: Crabtree, 1985.

Kraus, Robert. *Herman the Helper*. New York: Prentice-Hall Books, 1974.

Morris, Ann. *Loving*. New York: Lothrop, Lee & Shepard Books, 1990.

Munsch, Robert. *Love You Forever*. Scarborough, Ontario, Canada: Firefly Books, 1987.

Williams, Vera B. *A Chair for My Mother*. New York: Greenwillow Books, 1982.

Forgiveness and Telling Lies: Books

Ganz, Yaffa. *Sharing a Sunshine*. New York: Feldheim Publishers, 1989.

Marshall, James. *George and Martha*. Boston: Houghton Mifflin, 1972.

McKissack, Patricia C. *The Honest-to-Goodness Truth*. New York: Atheneum Books for Young Readers, 2000.

Shannon, David. *No, David!* New York: Blue Sky Press, 1998.

Jealously and Envy: Books

Ganz, Yaffa. *The Story of Mimmy and Simmy*. New York: Feldheim Publishers, 2000.

Henkes, Kevin. *Chester's Way*. New York: Greenwillow Books, 1988.